two fleas & no dog

transform your marriage from FLEADOM to FREEDOM

by
CRAIG HILL

FAMILY FOUNDATIONS INTERNATIONAL
LITTLETON COLORADO
WWW.FAMILYFOUNDATIONS.COM

Family Foundations International
P.O. Box 320
Littleton, Colorado 80160

Printed in the United States of America

All Scripture quotations are taken from The New King James
Bible unless otherwise noted: *The New King James Bible*,
Thomas Nelson Publishers, 1982; *The New American Standard
Bible*, The Lockman Foundation, 1960, 1962, 1963, 1968, 1971,
1973, 1975

*The characters in many of the examples cited in this book
are real life people whom the author has known. For their
privacy, however, their names and some of the insignificant
details have been altered. Alternatively, some incidents
described are not sequential events, but are composites of
several incidents; nevertheless, they reflect very real
situations.*

dedication

To my wife, Jan, the treasure of whose company God has blessed me to share in this life. Because of her, our marriage has truly become a fulfilling and delightful daily experience. Jan actually did teach me to paddle a canoe without tipping it over.

acknowledgements

I want to give special thanks to:

Arabelle Hinchliff for typesetting and editing.
Colleen Dudley for editing.
Jan McCoy and Pastor Byron Newby for their editorial
suggestions.
Jason Dudley for cover graphics design.

endorsements

Sam & Linda Caster

Craig Hill has an incredible gift for identifying the simple and basic truths in very complex situations. In this book, *Two Fleas and No Dog*, Craig has insightful views on the dynamics of marriage. He offers not only a clear meaning of marriage through the perspective of covenant, but provides very practical means of dealing with some of the most threatening issues that plague most marriages such as miscommunication, conflict resolution and how and why to forgive each other.

This book flows like an owner's manual in the dynamics of marriage. Our recommendation: read it, use it, and give it to others—especially your own children. We have personally benefited from Craig's work; it's a true gift.

Sam & Linda Caster
CEO of Mannatech and Founders of MannaRelief Ministries
Dallas, Texas (www.mannarelief.org)

Leo & Molly Godzich

For many years, Craig and Jan Hill have been leading articulators of the value of covenant as it relates to marriage. This book is an eye-opening, life-changing explanation of how to overcome common misunderstandings and increase transparency, intimacy and overall marital joy. We are thrilled to recommend you read it and apply its wealth of wisdom to your marriage!

Dr. Leo & Molly Godzich
NAME—National Association of Marriage Enhancement
Phoenix, Arizona (www.nameonline.net)

Bob & Audrey Meisner

Craig Hill is an expert in communicating covenant. Applying the truths found in this book will result in a newfound freedom in your marriage relationship that you never dreamed possible!

You'll be refreshed! Revived! And rekindled as you grasp the concept of selfless love and its eternal rewards. Over the many years of working with Craig and Jan and Family Foundations International, we are convinced that they conduct some of the most life-changing seminars available. Craig Hill is an exceptional Bible teacher, mining God's true treasures for such a time as this. We highly recommend this book.

Bob & Audrey Meisner
Authors of Bestseller, *Marriage Under Cover*
Phoenix, Arizona (www.bobandaudrey.com)

Additional Resources are listed at the end of each chapter. Unless noted, resources are by Craig Hill. Resources are available through Family Foundations International. You may locate the FFI office nearest you through www.familyfoundations.com on the Internet.

 Books   Audio CDs   DVDs   Seminars/Courses

---

contents

introduction

Perspectives

As I begin this introduction, I would first like to clarify a couple of personal perspectives from which I have written this book. In reality, I don't think that it is ever possible for a writer to be truly objective. Any author will write from the perspective of his own personal experience and worldview. Consequently, I would like to share with you up front the perspectives from which I am writing. Most of what I have learned about marriage relationship has come out of my personal experience in my own marriage and in interacting with others.

As you progress through the book, you will find that I frequently refer to experiences I have had or understandings I have gained through my relationship with God. While it is not my intent to impose upon you my view of God and relationship with Him, I also make no apology for the fact that my experience and understanding is rooted in dynamic, interactive relationship with the God of the Bible, and it is from this perspective that I share my thoughts with you.

Secondly, throughout this book, I will frequently refer to passages found in the Bible. This is because I have discovered that there are many principles found in the Bible that simply describe how life works. I understand that many Christians have used the Bible as a rulebook by which they condemn others, tell others what to believe, or how they should live their lives. We have all met such people. I have never enjoyed having other people condemn me or tell me what to do, and probably neither have you. So, my goal in citing various Bible passages is not to judge, condemn or control, but rather to impart to you the life-descriptive principle that will help you in your marriage. Jan and I have found that when these principles are understood and followed, they can reduce the level of pain and torment, and significantly enhance the fulfillment experienced in marriage as we progress through life.

Rules vs. Principles

To understand the difference between a principle and a rule, let me contrast these two concepts:

Principle: Gravity works everywhere on planet earth 24/7 and will attract any object within the atmosphere rapidly towards the earth's surface.

Rule: Do not dive into the shallow end of the swimming pool.

In this case, the rule is probably based at least in part on a principle. However, in order to have a less pain-filled experience of life, it is far more critical that you understand and abide by the principle than simply by the rule. If you understand the principle of gravity, you may be able to break the rule and dive into the shallow end of the pool without being hurt. However, if you mistake the principle for a rule and think you can violate the principle of gravity without consequence, you will inevitably be hurt. If you truly do not understand the principle of gravity, and consequently you regularly step off tall buildings and cliffs, this behavior will definitely affect your quality of life, and you will experience significantly more pain than someone who understands and abides by the principle of gravity.

Let me give you another example. You may hear the rule, "Don't stick a paper clip or metal knife blade into an electric wall outlet." If you don't understand and believe the principle that electric current is powerful and dangerous when directly contacted by humans, you may reject the rule as someone trying to control you or impose their personal values upon you. By rejecting the rule, you may choose to poke the paper clip into the hot lead in the wall outlet. However, because of the principle that electricity really is powerful and deadly, you will experience much more pain (or even death) if you do so than someone who understands and abides by the principle expressed in what you thought was just an arbitrary rule.

Just like principles of gravity or electricity, we have discovered in the Bible many principles that describe how life works regarding marriage and human relationships. Some people seem to regularly violate these principles that others understand and walk in. As a result, those who understand and abide by these principles tend to experience marriage as emotionally pleasurable and deeply fulfilling, while those who reject or violate these principles tend to experience marriage as an unfulfilling, emotionally painful, endurance contest. So in this book, we want to examine some key principles and processes that will help us move our marriage from the endurance contest stages to the fulfilling, pleasurable experience that marriage was intended to be.

In concluding this introduction, let me summarize for you three key principles we have found to be critical to marriage. I will note for each point both the challenge and the solution to implement for each principle. Since the implementation of these principles is a powerful key to unlock freedom in marriage, we will go into much more detail on these three necessary components in subsequent chapters.

It is important to understand that these three principles are sequential, and build upon each other. As you move through the chapters of this book, I believe you may be confronted with some of your own hidden fears and insecurities. It may then be a challenge not to deny, hide, or run from these, but rather to bring them into the light, and take some steps to secure personal freedom in those areas. **When all three of these principles are functionally in place in a marriage, most couples experience a renewed sense of romantic love for one another, and a deep sense of security and fulfillment in their marriage relationship.** There is also tremendous joy in knowing that they are accomplishing together a purpose designed by God that is far greater than themselves and their own personal pleasure.

Here are the three principles:

A. Covenant: Marriage: a Unilateral, Unconditional Blood Covenant

Challenge: Because we do not live in a covenant culture and most people have not been taught in any context the nature and value of a covenant, society in general has exchanged the value of marriage as a covenant for the value of marriage as a contract. This breeds insecurity and independence in marriage relationship.

Solution: Put the protective hedge of covenant back in place around your marriage by understanding and committing to covenant.

B. Communication: Regular, Transparent, Heart to Heart

Challenge: a) Due to the insecurity of contract marriage, many couples are afraid to be totally open and transparent with each other in communication. Hidden things in the heart then block true transparency and thus intimacy.

b) Lack of understanding or awareness of spiritual warfare in marital communication results in couples fighting each other instead of fighting the true enemy.

c) In addition, due to a lack of awareness of the relational level of communication, most couples miscommunicate on this level and consequently deeply wound each other without ever becoming aware of how the wound occurred. As a result, they then have no ability to deal with or heal these wounds.

Solution: a) Establish regular open, transparent heart to heart communication within the security of covenant marriage.

b) Understand and recognize spiritual warfare in communication and become each other's ally against the true enemy.

c) Become aware of the relational level of communication and regularly bring healing to the wounds that are inadvertently created.

C. Conflict: Effective Strategy for Conflict Resolution

Challenge: Due to a lack of regular, effective, transparent heart to heart communication, and the wounding of relational miscommunication, most couples have no foundation for communication and thus find no success in resolving conflict. No effective strategy is developed, and so conflict just becomes too painful for many couples to resolve. They simply learn to avoid it.

Solution: Learn to utilize conflict to identify root causes of fears, insecurities, and lies in the heart. Then implement a process to effectively replace these compelling root causes with love, security, and truth in the heart. Then implement an effective strategy to resolve the conflict with these other factors removed.

chapter 1

Flea VS Free

B ill, I've discovered your problem," I exclaimed. "The root problem in your marriage is that you're a flea. If you'd just stop being selfish, everything in your marriage would be fine." Those were the words I jokingly told my friend, Bill, who had been struggling in his marriage for some years. Even though I spoke these words in a good-humored, joking manner, we both knew that the words were true. Bill and his wife were indeed both fleas. As with so many couples I have met, the primary problem for my friend Bill was not that he was unaware of his "fleadom." The basic problem was that Bill did not yet know how, or have the emotional reserve to stop being a flea in relationship to his wife.

If the truth were known, I think that every one of us would have to admit that in at least some areas of our lives and marriage relationship we personally really do think and behave like fleas. No one can truthfully say, "I am free in every area of my marriage relationship." In the early years of my own marriage, I was certain that I was not a flea, but instead I was a really kind, considerate, longsuffering, loving husband. Whatever problems were in our marriage, I was quite convinced, were due to dysfunctional areas in my wife, Jan's, life. Consequently, several of the early years of our marriage were not pleasant or enjoyable, but rather quite miserable. It really wasn't until seven years into our marriage that I began to take stock of my own selfishness and realize how much of a flea I really was toward Jan. It was at this point that our marriage really began to be transformed from fleadom to freedom. I will share more of our own personal journey with you in chapter five.

Although neither Jan nor I have any formal training nor degrees in marriage counseling, psychology, or theology, we have had opportunity to listen to and pray for many couples over the years. When we first got an understanding of the key principle of relational communication that is shared in chapter six, our marriage was so dramatically transformed, that many people who knew us began to ask what had happened. Consequently, we began to share with other couples these same principles and processes that had so helped our marriage relationship.

After a few years of one on one counseling and praying for couples, we began to hold seminars for small groups of couples, and in so doing stumbled into a ministry process that has since proven to be life changing for many individuals and couples. Through this ministry process we have seen, for many individuals, the compelling forces that drive certain dysfunctional and destructive attitudes and behavior totally eliminated and replaced at the core of the being.

When even just one partner in a marriage experiences a core transformation from fleadom to freedom in a particular area of life, such as security of personal value or welfare as discussed below, this dramatically changes the dynamics of that marriage for the better. These initial seminars conducted in 1987 were the beginning of the ministry organization we now head, called Family Foundations International (FFI). As a result of the demand for such seminars, we have now trained teams in North America and many other countries around the world that conduct these same *Ancient Paths Seminars*, utilizing this same ministry process, and experiencing these same results. You may wish to check the FFI website for more information on *Ancient Paths Seminars* conducted in your local area.[1]

Fleadom vs. Freedom

I have chosen to utilize the analogy of being a flea to describe the areas of selfishness with which we all must deal in our own marriage relationship. While there may be many areas of your marriage in which you don't relate to your spouse as a flea, everyone will find at least a few areas of "fleadom," which when transformed into freedom will dramatically affect the quality of life experienced by both partners in the marriage. Having said this, let's look at some definitions of these words.

Flea: (flē) *n.* "Any member of 1600 species and sub-species of small, wingless, bloodsucking (parasitic) insects (order of Siphonaptera) found from the Arctic Circle to the Arabian deserts. *Specialized anatomical structures allow the **flea** to attach itself to the skin of mammals or birds and consume their blood.*" [2]

Fleadom: (flē´dǝm) *n.* **1:** The quality or state of relating to a marriage partner as a flea would relate to a dog. **a:** Relating to a spouse in a parasitic manner, with a primary concern for meeting the needs of self while holding little to no regard for the well being of the spouse. **exp. b:** The art of viewing one's spouse as a

---

[1] See Appendix. For more information on seminars in your local area, visit the Internet site: www.familyfoundations.com

[2] Encyclopedia Britannica Online

host, whose primary purpose is to meet the sexual, emotional, financial, physical, intellectual, spiritual, recreational and any other needs of the flea. (Author's Definition)

Freedom: (frē´dƏm) *n.* **1:** The quality or state of being free; as **a:** the absence of necessity, coercion, or constraint in choice or action **b:** liberation from slavery or restraint or from the power of another.[3]

So what is the difference between a free man and a flea man? (On occasion throughout the course of the book, I will use the generic term "man" or "he" to denote mankind, male or female, so as to avoid the need to utilize "his/her" or "he/she." If I am speaking about something uniquely pertinent to a male or female, I will so denote.) A person who is a flea values his own survival above all else, while a free person may have several other core values, such as his God, his integrity, his word and his family, which are to him more precious than his own life. A free person is not compelled by his own present need, but rather is free to deny or defer present need for the sake of a longer-term value, while a flea person is always compelled by the fulfillment of present personal need. A free person makes choices based on deeply held values, while a flea person makes choices primarily in response to the choices of the host. I have summarized some of the differences I have observed in the following chart.

> A free person is not compelled by his own present need...

---

3 Merriam-Webster Online Dictionary

FLEA	FREE
Personal survival takes priority above all else	Deeply held core values take priority over personal survival
Compelled by present need	Free to defer or deny present need
Compelled to make choices in reaction to the host	Free to make choices based on deeply held core values
Compelled to react behaviorally to circumstances and choices of others	Free to initiate new behavior based on goals and values
Controlled by the sins and weaknesses of others, especially the host	Free to bless others even in their sins and weaknesses
Only able to see and choose for short-term, immediate fulfillment of self	Free to see and choose either short-term or long-term fulfillment of others or self
Can conditionally love others only when doing so means little or no pain or inconvenience for self	Free to love others, meaning to choose the highest good for all concerned even at the cost of personal pain or suffering

Fleadom Rooted in Identity and Welfare Fears

In moving your marriage from fleadom to freedom, the greatest battle you will face will probably be dealing with two primary fears and insecurities. These two compelling forces are usually deep-rooted in the heart and drive much of our external fleaish attitudes and behavior. The first powerfully compelling force that drives most people is a deep-seated, sometimes unconscious fear of not being loved or valuable.

Secondly, many people also experience a deep-rooted fear of not having their needs met. Fear always compels people to attempt to eliminate that which is perceived to be causing the fear. **These two root fears regarding identity ("I'm not valuable") and welfare ("My needs won't be met") compel many people to behave as intensely self-focused fleas attempting to become valuable and to meet their own needs.** Below is a very pertinent Bible passage instructing us to deal with these two specific areas of fleadom (selfishness).

"Do nothing from selfishness or empty conceit, but with humility of mind let each of you regard one another as more important than himself; do not merely look out for your own personal interests, but also for the interests of others" (Philippians 2:3-4 NASB).

Our own inability to do these things should actually be an indicator to us of our own bondage to fleadom and need to get free. Firstly, we are told to do <u>nothing</u> from selfishness or empty conceit. Of course, only a truly free person can do this.

Next we are instructed to <u>regard another, in this case your spouse, as more important than yourself</u>. Why is this so hard to do? This has to do with the identity fear we were discussing above. If you are convinced that you are unconditionally loved and that your value is secure independent of your performance, then it may be possible for you to consider your spouse as more important than yourself. On the other hand, if in the depths of your own heart you don't feel truly loved and valuable, then it is very likely that you will unconsciously be compelled to seek your own value. Insecurity regarding your personal value will motivate you to be very performance-oriented and to continually seek to do those things that you think will bring value to your life.

Only when your own heart becomes secure in the fact that you are loved by God, and therefore truly valuable, will you be free to choose to make another person more valuable than yourself. Until that actually happens in your heart (not just your mind), you will be compelled to devalue you spouse and be consumed pursuing those things that you believe will bring value to you in the sight of others, or at least in you own sight.

> Only when your own heart becomes secure in the fact that you are loved by God, and therefore truly valuable, will you be free to choose to make another person more valuable than yourself.

Consequently, if you observe that you have great difficulty considering your spouse as more valuable than yourself, you will never change this by trying harder to value him. Your own heart won't let you. Your lack of valuing your spouse is only an indicator of the fact that you are not secure in God's love and in your inherent value. This is primarily remedied by an encounter with God in which He removes the deep lie and insecurity from your heart and replaces it with an intense feeling of His love and of your inherent value in His sight. This is not just a theory. Jan and I have seen this actually happen experientially for many people to whom we have ministered.

The third part of the instruction from the above passage is to look out for the interests of others (my spouse), even above your own personal interests. Again, the problem ensues when you are not secure in the fact that your own personal interests will be taken care of. If your personal welfare is at stake, you cannot consider the interests of another ahead of your own. Again, your own heart won't let you. If you don't believe that there is anyone greater than yourself who loves you and will take care of you, then your own heart will compel you to take care of yourself ahead of others. If life experience in the past has proven to you that no one else will be there for you, or you have been deeply wounded, abused, or violated in some way, then you will probably be compelled, even unconsciously, to look after your own personal interests and to protect yourself.

On the other hand, if you are truly secure that your needs will be met, and your personal welfare is not at stake, then you can rest inside and be secure in knowing that God will meet your needs and take care of your interests. When this is true, you can choose to consider your spouse's interests and welfare ahead of your own.

So, again if you observe that you have great difficulty considering the interests of your spouse above your own, you will never change this by trying harder to consider his interests above yours. Your inability to do this should be an indicator to you that you have a deep-rooted fear in your heart that God won't meet your needs and consequently you must look after yourself. Fortunately, Jan and I have seen many times a total inner transformation of heart in seminar small groups we have conducted, as that root of that fear was identified, eliminated and replaced with a deep sense of true security and trust that God will take care of the personal interests. When this has happened, that person has then transformed in that area from fleadom to freedom and the entire marriage relationship in that area was radically changed.

In looking at the above symptoms of fleadom in marriage, most people still don't recognize their own selfishness. Many people really believe that they may have some minor area of fleadom to deal with, but by and large they are really pretty free. And of course most of us are convinced that the person to whom we are married is much more of a flea. "I, of course, am the loving, giving host (dog)." **However, it is almost universally true that fleas don't marry dogs, but rather fleas marry other fleas. True dogs aren't attracted to fleas.** Thus if your spouse is a flea, well...?

Hence the title, *Two Fleas and No Dog*.

Reflection

1. In my marriage relationship in general, am I a flea, or am I free? (Please refer to comparison table on page 11.)

2. Am I secure enough in God's love and the knowledge that I am valuable and my needs will be met so that I can:

   a. regard my spouse as more important than myself and

   b. look out for the interests of my spouse ahead of my own personal interests?

Resources

 The Ancient Paths

 The Ancient Paths (book on audio)

4Stages of Marriage

In interacting with numerous couples throughout the years, I believe that it is important for any couple to first take stock of the current state of their marriage relationship. In order to help you assess this, I have described below a model we have used consisting of four stages of relationship. It is important to recognize that none of these stages are permanent, but couples can always move from one stage to another. How rapidly you are able to move forward in your marriage from fleadom to freedom will greatly depend upon which one of these stages more accurately describes your present relationship.

Since many couples seem to have little or no awareness of the true status of their relationship, in an attempt to move forward in their marriage, some couples in Stages 1 or 2 immediately attempt to pursue activities that require the trust and emotional maturity of a Stage 4 relationship. When they then fail, they once again blame each other and conclude that their situation is hopeless. This, of course is not at all the case. They simply needed to more accurately assess the reality of their present level of trust and emotional maturity and then move forward a little more slowly.

In his book, *The Seven Habits of Highly Effective People*, Steven Covey outlined an emotional maturity continuum consisting of three phases, dependence, independence, and interdependence[1]. I believe that we could also add another stage, codependence, which actually is degeneration backwards from the initial dependence stage. These four phases of emotional maturity help define the four stages of marital relationship that we have observed.

It is evident that a baby starts out in a state of emotional dependence, a victim, totally at the mercy of others, and life is all about <u>you</u> doing something to meet my needs. An unhealthy child may regress backwards in emotional maturity to the stage of co-dependence. In this stage he is intensely focused on getting needs met at any cost, particularly at the expense of others around him.

> For the interdependent person, life is all about God and us.

Deprivation, violation, and emotional trauma and wounding in childhood help to facilitate this movement backwards into intense fleadom.

The emotionally healthy child grows into the stage of emotional independence, becomes confident in his own abilities, doesn't need others any more, and life now becomes all about <u>me</u> meeting my own needs. None of these first three stages of maturity have much awareness of the needs of others around. An emotionally healthy person may then mature into the stage of

---

[1] Covey, Steven, *The Seven Habits of Highly Effective People*, New York, NY, Simon and Schuster 1989, p. 49

interdependence, in which he is at peace inside, trusting that his own needs will be met by God, Who loves him. This person is then free to focus on meeting the needs of others and fulfilling a purpose beyond self that includes working together with others. For the interdependent person, life is all about <u>God</u> and <u>us</u>. Let's now look at how this emotional maturity continuum is reflected in the following four stages of marriage relationship. As you read the descriptions, ask yourself which picture most accurately describes your current situation.

Stage 1: Two Fleas and No Dog

Most couples when they first marry can be likened to two fleas. A flea is a small parasitic animal looking for a large host animal upon which it can feed. A large majority of people when they marry, like a flea, are focused on finding someone who will meet their needs and desires. When Steve met Nancy, she seemed to be exactly what he had always been looking for in a woman. She was so beautiful, had such a great personality, and was so fun to be with. She was the perfect "dog" for this flea. He was not focused on how he could bless her, meet her needs and desires, give to her, or honor her. Although he did some of these things, his focus was truly on how she was perfect to meet his needs and desires. Without realizing it, Steve believed that he had found the perfect "dog" who was so full of the life he needed that he could just keep drawing that life from her and she wouldn't even miss it.

When Nancy met Steve, he too seemed to be the perfect man for her. He was her "Prince Charming"–so strong, kind, courteous, and handsome. He was everything she has ever hoped for in a man. He also was a huge "dog" for this flea. Nancy's focus was not on how she could bless Steve, give to him, honor him, and meet his needs and desires. Her focus was on how he could meet her needs and desires. Nancy felt so safe and secure around Steve, and it seemed that she could share anything with him and he never closed her off or said anything

19

unkind. He was so full of the life that she needed that she could just keep drawing that life from him and he didn't even miss it.

During their premarital relationship, both Steve and Nancy were on their best behavior, still in the process of wooing each other. Neither of them realized that they were both fleas. The perception of each was that the other was so full of life that he would never run out. So, Steve and Nancy got married. Soon afterward, they each began to discover that their marriage partner was not full of infinite life and maybe was not the large "dog" previously supposed. As a matter of fact, as time went on, Steve discovered that Nancy was not a "dog" at all, but in reality she was a flea looking to him to meet her every need. Nancy likewise discovered that Steve, too was not a "dog" at all, but rather he was also a flea looking to her to meet his every need.

Now in reality, we **have a relationship comprised of two fleas and no dog**. Each flea has been deceived into believing that the other is a dog, full of infinite emotional life. Both fleas are busy trying to suck the emotional life out of each other, and no one has any more life to give. Now discouragement, disappointment, shattered dreams and hopelessness began to set in for both Steve and Nancy regarding their marriage relationship.

Life for the flea is all about how <u>you</u> affect me. The flea is totally focused on changing the other person. My life revolves around what <u>you</u> do or don't do. "If <u>you</u> would change, this marriage would work." "If <u>you</u> would stop doing this, or start doing that, everything would be fine." "The problem is that <u>you</u> are selfish." "<u>You</u> keep doing destructive things that hurt me." The flea never takes responsibility for any of his own choices, but is continually focused upon the choices of the spouse. The choices of the marriage partner actually determine the well being of the flea each day.

The flea is convinced that if he just tells the marriage partner all of her problems, then these problems will be recognized, changed and everything will be fine. One husband I know actually presented his wife with a written list of more than 47 ways she had hurt him in the last several months, thinking that she would immediately see all the things she had done wrong and change. For some reason, this wife didn't respond the way her husband had hoped, and needless to say, his marriage was not benefited through this letter. The actual problem, of course is the selfishness of the flea looking to the spouse to change and meet all of his needs. Listen to your own language and even how you read this book. Are your thoughts immediately drawn to how you must change, or are they drawn to wanting your spouse to get this and change? Just this observation alone may help you to take stock of the reality of your life and marriage relationship.

Stage 2: Two Drowning People In Open Water

After marrying as two fleas, neither Steve nor Nancy ever recognized or took responsibility for his or her own personal fleadom. Consequently, both became convinced that the problem in the marriage was the selfishness of the other person. Both Steve and Nancy continued to focus upon "you meeting my needs;" "how you have hurt me;" and "if you really loved me, if you really cared, you would change." This then caused much more frustration and emotional wounding for both Steve and Nancy. As a result, their marriage relationship then degenerated from being one of two fleas, to more that of two drowning people in close proximity to one another.

For the drowning person, life is now even more intensely about how <u>you</u> affect me. However, the feeling is now one of **desperation**. It now feels like, "If <u>you</u> don't change immediately, I'm going to perish (emotionally, spiritually, or sometimes even physically.)" "<u>You</u> are the cause of my drowning." "This is all <u>your fault</u>." In this stage, it becomes a matter of emotional survival. When I feel like I am drowning, I will do whatever I must do in order to get my needs met. I am desperate

21

for oxygen. In this condition, I am totally oblivious to the needs of anyone else around me, least of all my spouse. I just want my spouse to do what I need him to do immediately so that I can survive. The drowning stage is actually a step backward in emotional maturity from the flea stage.

It is very dangerous to be in the open water near a drowning person. This person is desperate, and if you get near him, he will climb on top of you and push you under the water, potentially drowning you in an attempt to stay above water and breath. In this stage both husband and wife have been deeply wounded and are desperate for emotional oxygen. They have now become each other's enemy. However, even marriage relationships that have degenerated to this stage are not beyond hope. We have seen relationships restored even from this stage of desperation, when couples have been willing to seek help.

Stage 3: Two Independent Swimmers Swimming Near Each Other

Larry and Barb both married as fleas just as Steve and Nancy did. However, within the first couple of years of marriage, Larry and Barb received some marriage counseling and began to recognize their own selfishness and "you" focus. They both realized that they could never improve their marriage by blaming each other, so they began to take personal responsibility for their own choices. However, neither Larry nor Barb really developed a trust for each other, nor did they develop a common purpose for their marriage together. Consequently, although they no longer looked to each other to meet their own needs, they grew apart and both became quite self-sufficient and independent.

While Larry and Barb were no longer fleas, and they certainly weren't drowning each other, their marriage developed into a relationship that could be described as two people independently swimming near each other, but not really swimming together or moving in any particular direction. Both of them were "I" centered. They were no longer blaming each other for their problems and pressuring each other to change. They each had now moved into a position of independence, looking only to self to meet needs. They each had their own set of friends.

Although both Larry and Barb had a relationship with the Lord, Barb really considered herself farther ahead of Larry spiritually. She had many friends who enjoyed the same spiritual pursuits that she did and spent much time in Bible study, prayer and conversation with her friends. Since Larry felt cut out of Barb's life spiritually and couldn't compete with all of her "spiritual" friends, he threw himself more into his work and his children. These were both areas in which Larry excelled and found affirmation.

Barb tended to be a night person, who would stay up late talking with friends and pursuing activities. Larry, on the other hand was a morning person, who liked to get up early and get his day started. These habits, coupled with past wounding, independence and self sufficiency in both made it difficult for Larry and Barb to even find a time to daily talk and pray with each other, or to pursue physical intimacy.

Larry longed to connect and feel loved and accepted by his wife, but it seemed that there was always an underlying message of "you don't measure up" coming at him from Barb. Barb, on the other hand, longed to be supported, protected and made to feel of high priority to Larry, but instead, it seemed that Larry always supported others and valued the opinions of others ahead of her. Consequently, their marriage was stuck in Stage 3.

For the independent swimmer, marriage relationship is all about me. "I can meet my own needs." "I don't really need you." "It doesn't really matter whether you change or not, because I will be fine whether you are or not." "My wellbeing is not dependent upon what you do or don't do, but rather upon the choices I make."

Independent swimmers in marriage tend to drift farther and farther apart as time goes on. Often times they find themselves in reality living like "married singles." They live in the same house, but truly have very little in common in their lives. Many times, in this stage, conflict is never resolved, and sometimes rarely even manifested. Both parties just learn how to avoid conflict and bury emotions. While the independent swimmer has moved a step forward in emotional maturity from the initial flea stage, there is still no synergy or common purpose to the marriage relationship, as was God's design.

Stage 4: Two Free Teammates In a Canoe Together Heading Toward a Common Goal

Eric and Leslie both committed their lives to Christ during teen-age years. They both realized that their identity needed to be complete in their relationship with God, not in looking for a marriage partner. Consequently, both Eric and Leslie made a decision during high school years not to engage in the traditional dating (girlfriend/boyfriend) system. They each decided that they wanted to reserve their heart only to be given to the person that God had intended for them to marry, not to multiple other people on the way. As a result, when Eric and Leslie married, they were able to begin their relationship and their marriage as teammates sitting in a canoe with an assigned destiny from God toward which to paddle.

When both husband and wife are secure in their own identities and are convinced that their needs are met by God, each are then able to begin to be concerned for blessing the other and for meeting a common goal synergistically. In this analogy, the canoe is the marriage itself, and there is a trust between the two partners in the canoe that neither of them will act for self against the other or toward the destruction of the canoe. Eric and Leslie Ludy are a real-life couple who have written a book about how the Lord led them together and prepared them for marriage. You may want to pick up their book entitled, *His Perfect Faithfulness.*[2] Eric & Leslie are now in ministry helping young people.[3]

For the two teammates in the canoe, life is about "God" and about "us." It is no longer about you or about me, but rather about us. Both husband and wife see accomplishing God's goal for the marriage and the team as far more important than that of the individual. This is really only possible when both partners are secure in the fact that they are inherently valuable and can trust God to meet their personal needs and desires. They can then both concentrate on learning how to maneuver the canoe together, learning how to balance, paddle and the other skills that are necessary for them to learn as a team to move the canoe toward the destination. "We" centered couples recognize their need for each other in order to accomplish the goal, but never look to each other as a source of life. They have learned to become dependent upon God alone, and interdependent toward each other.

Stage 4 couples have made a choice to identify and live for a common purpose and destiny greater than themselves. They realize that they are here to accomplish God's purpose for their lives, not their own purposes. While couples in the prior stages have no purpose to life or marriage greater than pain avoidance, personal happiness, pleasure and the fulfillment of self, this is not so for a free Stage 4 couple. Each of them has a far greater concern for the fulfillment of their God-given destiny and purpose than they do for the meeting of their individual personal needs. Their personal goals are all subservient to the common purpose for which they live. Great personal fulfillment and pleasure seem to be natural byproducts of a married couple

---

[2] Ludy, Eric and Leslie, *His Perfect Faithfulness*, Littleton, CO, Family Foundations Publishing, 1996

[3] Eric & Leslie Ludy. Internet website: www.ericandleslie.com

working together as a team to overcome challenges, defeat enemies, accomplish goals and pursue their destiny.

When a couple first finds their purpose and finally gets into the canoe, since they have not previously ridden in a canoe together, that couple will usually tip the canoe over a few times as they learn how to balance and paddle. In the beginning, a couple may experience times in which they are very uncoordinated in their paddling. Perhaps they may find themselves going round and round in circles or veering off to one side or the other as they are learning. However, because of their common goal and purpose, and their trust God, this couple is able to persevere through the learning process until they become very good as a team at moving their canoe forward toward the destination. Even though this couple may still face storms, whirlpools, and rapids in the river that may upset their canoe, they have learned to work together as a team to right the canoe and carry on toward the destination.

Another analogy I would like to employ for this fourth stage of marriage is that of two rechargeable batteries. This is the opposite of the flea type of relationship. In this analogy, God is the re-charger, and each person is like a rechargeable battery. Both husband and wife are looking to the Lord as the source of emotional life and are drawing their strength and life from Him.

Each partner in this relationship is relating to his spouse as a battery would relate to an appliance, such as a CD player. The job of the battery is simply to provide life to the CD player. When the battery runs out of life, it does not look to the CD player to provide life. The battery does not say, "Hey, CD player, I have been putting out a lot of life to you recently, and I think that I deserve to get something back." No, when the battery runs out of life, it goes back to the re-charger (God) to receive more life. When it is all charged up again, it then goes back to the CD player and once again plugs in to provide more life.

Can you imagine what a marriage relationship would be like if both partners considered themselves to be rechargeable batteries designed to provide life to the CD player (spouse). In this case, both partners are complete in their own identities and are looking to God to meet their needs. Their focus is on meeting the needs of their marriage partner unconditionally and providing life, not meeting their own needs and taking life. In this scenario with two rechargeable batteries, there is an incredible synergy produced as life flows from God through both partners toward each other. When either or both run out of life, they don't look to each other to provide life, but rather go back to the re-charger for more life. Only couples who have learned to be rechargeable batteries get to sit in a canoe and paddle toward God's destiny for their marriage.

> ...there is an incredible synergy produced as life flows from God through both partners toward each other.

I believe that this battery theory of relationship is how God intended for marriage to be from the very beginning. Unfortunately, in our society, the present "dating system" practiced by most people teaches people to be selfish fleas. This system teaches people to look for someone who "looks good to me, makes me feel good, and meets my needs and desires." I then engage this person to be my "boyfriend" or "girlfriend" and use them to satisfy my emotional needs until they no longer please me, at which time I discard them and find someone else I can "be with" to please myself. This flea training system then becomes our primary practice and strategy to prepare young people for marriage. No wonder most people in reality marry as selfish fleas, and our national divorce rate is greater than fifty percent.

Having briefly outlined these four stages of marriage, the obvious question for you is, "In which stage is your marriage currently functioning?" Listen to the thoughts and words you express regarding your own marriage partner. Honestly assess your own heart toward your marriage partner. I know that someone will say, "I am in the canoe trusting God to move toward our destiny, but my husband keeps tipping the canoe over." This wife talking about what her husband is doing or not doing in the marriage is still "you" centered, and is obviously in Stage 1 or Stage 2.

God's plan is for every marriage to move into Stage 4 and function there. The good news is that while we have seen many couples struggle in each of the first three stages for years, when they have embraced and implemented the principles contained in this book, many have cooperated with God in moving their marriages into the fourth stage. We have actually seen drowning people first learn to float, then to swim, and ultimately to paddle a canoe together with their partner toward a destination. No matter in what stage you currently find your marriage, the three key principles expressed in the following chapters will help move your marriage further down the path toward fulfilling the purpose for which God called you together as a married couple.

> No matter in what stage you currently find your marriage, the three key principles expressed in the following chapters will help move your marriage further down the path toward fulfilling the purpose for which God called you together as a married couple.

Warning: If you determine that your marriage is currently in Stage 1 or 2, it may be very difficult to implement the principles and do the practice exercises suggested in the following chapters without some outside help. This book alone may not be enough to help you breakthrough into freedom. You will probably need some help from others. I have found that many couples remain stuck in Stage 1 or 2 for many years simply due to the fact that they refuse to ask anyone for help. Sometimes a flea is so fearful of losing its perceived source of life that it doesn't want to disrupt anything in its current unhealthy, destructive ecosystem. Below are listed three very practical steps you may take to begin to move your marriage toward Stage 4.

1) If you are in Stage 1 or 2, or 3, the first step I would recommend toward freedom is to work on resolving the deep-rooted identity and welfare fears in each of you. We have developed experiential seminars released through Family Foundations International designed to deal with these issues. I would highly suggest that you look into attending an *Ancient Paths Seminar* or an *Overcoming Anger Seminar* at your earliest convenience. These seminars are offered throughout North America and in many other countries around the world. For a list of seminars near you visit our Internet website: www.familyfoundations.com[4].

2) **If you are in Stages 1 or 2, it is critical for you to ask for help** from your pastor, or find a counselor or mentor couple, who can help walk with you through the implementation of Covenant, Communication and Conflict Resolution. If you don't have a pastor or know of a counselor or mentor couple to help you, I would suggest contacting the National Association of Marriage Enhancement (NAME). You will find NAME Centers with Certified Marriage Specialists and marriage mentors in many cities.[5]

3) With your counselor or mentor couple, systematically work through the material and exercises contained in the remainder of this book.

---

[4] See Appendix. Find a seminar near you on the Internet site www.familyfoundations.com (Around the World)

[5] For further information on NAME see the Internet site www.nameonline.net

Even if you find your marriage in Stages 3 or 4, we have found that an *Ancient Paths Seminar* is still very beneficial. You may be able to work through the material and exercises contained in this book together as a couple without a counselor or mentor couple. However, if you get stuck or experience significant conflict, please seek out a counselor or mentor couple who can help you move forward. Let's now begin to look at the first principle regarding marriage as a covenant.

Reflection

In which stage do I find myself operating in my marriage most of the time? Listen to the thoughts and words you express regarding your own marriage partner. Honestly assess your own heart toward your marriage partner.

Stage 1: **Two Fleas and No Dog**: you focused; emotional dependence. Life is about blaming and accusing you for all of my problems.

Stage 2: **Two Drowning People In Open Water**: intensely you focused; emotional codependence; I desperately need you to meet my needs and demands and do what I want or I won't survive. My very survival is controlled by you.

Stage 3: **Two Independent Swimmers Swimming Near Each Other**: I focused; emotional independence. Life is about me taking care of myself independent of you.

Stage 4: **Two Free Teammates In a Canoe Together Heading Toward a Common Goal**: we focused; emotionally interdependent. Life is about the two of us together as a team finding and pursuing God's destiny and purpose for our marriage and lives.

Resources

[1] *An Ancient Paths Seminar*: Overcoming Anger or The Ancient Paths Seminar. See Appendix for details and www.familyfoundations.com for schedule of upcoming events.

(•) [1] The Courtship Course–God's Ancient Path to Romance & Marriage (See Appendix for details.)

🎧 Dating vs. Courtship

📖 His Perfect Faithfulness (Ludy)

chapter 3
Covenant
Protection

O ne hot summer morning, as a young boy of about 10, Don was sitting in the bleachers with a couple of his friends at the baseball diamond near his home taking in a baseball game.[1] His team was winning 5 to 2 and Don was really enjoying the game. He watched as the pitcher wound up and threw a fastball. Don watched the batter swing, and the next thing he knew, he was knocked backward off the bleacher and found himself lying on the wooden plank between the bleachers. The batter had sent a foul ball flying that hit Don right on the mouth.

---

[1] Sherman, Dean, *Relationships Series*, Kailua Kona, HI, PACU Video Productions, 1985. This example is based on an actual event as told by Dean Sherman in this video.

As he picked himself up off of the wooden floor, Don now became conscious of an excruciating pain in the front of his mouth. His friends tried to see what was wrong and to help Don. He knew that there was nothing they could do to help, so he took off running toward his home. As he ran, Don wondered what might have happened to cause such intense pain. If he moved his lips there was pain. If he moved his tongue, he felt intense pain. If he opened his mouth to breath there was intense pain. When he got home, Don yelled for his mom to come help, and he quickly ran into the bathroom to have a look in the mirror.

Don's mom arrived in the bathroom just as he got the light turned on and carefully opened his mouth to have a look at the damage done by the stray baseball. As he slowly opened his mouth, his mother shrieked and Don nearly passed out at the sight of what they both saw. The baseball had hit Don directly in the mouth and had broken off his left front tooth diagonally from top to bottom. There, dangling in the air beneath the remaining fang-like piece of tooth, was raw nerve. Now Don understood why he had experienced so much pain on the way home. When saliva, or his tongue or air or anything touched that raw nerve, it resulted in excruciating pain. Don's mother quickly took him to the dentist in order to remedy the problem.

Let's talk a little about Don's problem with the raw nerve dangling out of the tooth. Why did God create that nerve to produce so much pain? Did God make a mistake by making the nerve so sensitive? Is the problem really that the nerve is too sensitive? NO, the problem is that the nerve has been extended into an environment, which God never intended for it to experience. The nerve was designed by God to be very sensitive, but it was also designed to be encased within tooth enamel. If the protective tooth enamel is removed from around the nerve, then the nerve becomes exposed to an environment in which it was not designed to function. If that nerve continues to be exposed

34

it will begin to loose its sensitivity. If exposed outside the tooth for too long, it will loose all of its sensitivity and eventually die.

The heart or emotional make-up of men and women can be likened to the nerve in Don's tooth. God designed the heart to be very, very sensitive and delicate. However, the heart, like the nerve, was not designed to be exposed outside of the protection of covenant. Covenant is like the tooth, designed to protect something very delicate, and sensitive. When sexual intimacy or even just the depths of the heart is shared in a relationship before marriage, or even within marriage when the protection of covenant is not really intact, many times the pain experienced on a heart level is very similar to what Don experienced when the protective enamel of his tooth was missing.

Covenant was designed by God to be the protective covering around the heart like the tooth is to the nerve. Many people not understanding this, have opened and exposed the heart to an environment in which it is subject to severe pain and damage. Some people have done this numerous times and have hardened their own heart and deadened its sensitivity. When covenant is not properly in place within a marriage, often times each partner begins to develop enamel tooth material around their own heart to protect and insolate them from their partner. God's plan was for the tooth enamel to develop around both husband and wife, not between them. This then allows the sensitive vulnerable heart of each to be exposed to the other, within the protection of the tooth enamel (covenant) surrounding them both.

> Covenant was designed by God to be the protective covering around the heart

I believe that this analogy pictures the true meaning expressed in Genesis 2:24-25, *"Therefore a man shall leave his father and mother and be joined to his wife, and they shall become one flesh. And they were both naked, the man and his wife, and were not ashamed."* I believe that to be naked and not ashamed is not just referring to running about the garden without clothes on. No, but rather it is talking about being completely open, transparent, and vulnerable before each other without fear of shame, ridicule, criticism and wounding. It is the protective hedge of covenant that makes this possible within a marriage. We will talk much more about this in chapter seven.

What Is a Blood Covenant?

Since covenant is the God-ordained hedge around a marriage that is meant to protect the sensitive heart inside, let's begin to examine what a covenant is. The Bible is set in an eastern context, and much of the biblical presentation of God's relationship with man is couched in covenant terminology. Actually, I don't think that one can truly understand the Bible without understanding the concept of covenant. Covenant (often times referred to as "blood covenant") is an eastern, or tribal concept, which has been known and practiced for centuries in the East, but is neither known nor understood in the "civilized" West. If you had grown up in a tribal culture in Africa, North or South America, the Middle East, or Polynesia, you would probably still be somewhat familiar with the concept of covenant.

However, most of us have never seen anyone amongst our family or friends cut veins in their hands or arms, commingle the blood, drink the mixture and swear allegiance to one another unto death. The closest most of us have come to the concept of covenant is watching Geronimo make a blood covenant with another native Indian chief on TV when we were children. We then pricked our own finger with a friend and mixed the blood in order to become "blood brothers". In actuality, in our modern western culture, the value of covenant has by and large been exchanged for the value of contract. Our legal profession has made us familiar with this concept of contract. But what then is a covenant?

A blood covenant is a solemn agreement made between men in the presence of the deity in whom they believe, which can only be broken by death. Simply put, covenant is a promise that is broken only by death. **The primary characteristics of a blood covenant are: unilateral, unconditional and irrevocable.** I realize that there are many covenants in the Bible that are indeed conditional. However, we are talking here about the type of covenant that we have with God by the blood of Jesus Christ, which is depicted on earth by the marriage relationship between husband and wife. The New Covenant by the blood of Jesus is indeed unilateral, unconditional, and irrevocable.

A blood covenant is the closest, most sacred, most enduring, binding agreement known to men. A covenant is virtually never broken by those who understand and practice blood covenanting. It is such a sacred **commitment for which a man or woman would die before dishonoring himself in breaking his word.** In the East, a man's word in a vow or covenant is more valuable than his own life. A free man values his word above his life, while a flea man always values his own survival above all else, including his word. It is said that in the 19th century if a man ever broke a covenant in Africa, even his own relatives

> A blood covenant is the closest, most sacred, most enduring, binding agreement known to men.

would help hunt him down to kill him. He and his offspring would be hunted and killed for up to four generations for covenant breaking. I have heard it said that among North American native peoples a covenant breaker would be hunted and killed for up to seven generations.

The reason that it is so important for us to understand the serious nature of a covenant is that such thinking has all but disappeared from our western society today. A man's word has become quite meaningless today in much of society. Whereas in past times a covenant thinker would rather die than break his word, today a man would rather break his word than be inconvenienced to miss lunch.

I find that it is difficult today for people to understand that God is a covenant keeper and will keep His word. Most people can't relate to God keeping His word because they have no legitimate picture in human experience of someone who would keep his word even to his own detriment. In which segment of society should we look to see such an example? In the realm of politics? I read in history that there was a time in which a politician felt an obligation to fulfill his campaign promises no matter what the cost. In most countries, this is not common today.

How about in business? Again, there was a time in past history when a man gave his word that you could rely upon it. If he said it, he would do it, and a handshake was a reliable commitment. Today, a major part of the legal profession is engaged in writing agreements to try to bind men to their words. However, if a man has no value in his heart for his own word, the length and detail of the written agreement will not bind him. He will find a way to break his word and do what he wants.

In reality, only a truly free person has the ability to give his word and keep it no matter what. A flea is always dependent upon the actions and attitudes of others. Therefore a flea is driven by current unmet needs, circumstances and the choices of the host rather than by the internal integrity of his own word.

Marriage was designed by God to be a covenant entered into freely, not a contract entered into flealy. This is why we use covenant vows in the traditional marriage ceremony, binding ourselves in matrimony "until death us do part." This binding agreement that is to be broken only by the death of one or both of the parties was meant to provide a safe and secure environment in which the two could become one. However, if the free value of covenant (until death us do part) has been exchanged in society or personally for the flea value of contract (until adultery, abuse, abandonment, incompatibility, or someone perceived to be an upgrade shows up), then there is no protective tooth enamel surrounding the delicate hearts of the bride and groom. In seeking to restore the value of covenant to our own marriages it is important to really understand as easterners do, exactly what a covenant is.

H. Clay Trumbull, a biblical and anthropological scholar wrote a fascinating book in the late 1800s entitled, *The Blood Covenant*. In this work, Dr. Trumbull expounds upon the cultural traditions of blood covenanting in virtually every culture of the world. It was his thesis that God placed such traditions in each culture to prepare every people group in the world to understand the New Covenant God has made with man by the shedding of the blood of His Son, Jesus Christ. Below, I would like to quote a couple brief passages from Dr. Trumbull's book to give you an idea of how men in the past have made blood covenants with each other.

"In bringing this rite of the covenant of blood into new prominence, it may be well for me to tell of it as it was described to me by an intelligent native Syrian, who saw it consummated in a village at the base of the mountains of Lebanon.

It was two young men, who were to enter into this covenant. They had known each other, and had been intimate (he does not mean sexually) *for years; but now they were to become brother-friends, in the covenant of blood. Their relatives and neighbors were called together in the open place before the village fountain to witness the sealing compact. The young men publicly announced their purpose and their reasons for it. Their declarations were written down in duplicate—one paper for each friend—and signed by themselves and by several witnesses. One of the friends took a sharp lance, and opened a vein in the other's arm. Into the opening thus made he inserted a quill through which he sucked the living blood. The lancet-blade was carefully wiped on one of the duplicate covenant papers, and then it was taken by the other friend, who made a like incision in its first user's arm, and drank his blood through the quill, wiping the blade on the duplicate covenant-record. The two friends declared together, 'We are brothers in a covenant made before God: who deceiveth the other, him will God deceive.'*

39

Each blood-marked covenant-record was then folded carefully, to be sewed up in a small leathern case, or amulet, about an inch square; to be worn thenceforward by one of the covenant-brothers, suspended about the neck, or bound upon the arm, in token of **the indissoluble relation**[2] (See Exodus 13:16).

Dr. Trumbull further states: *"He who has entered into this compact with another, counts himself the possessor of a double life;* **for his friend, whose blood he has shared, is ready to lay down his life with him, or for him.**"[3] Dr. Trumbull then refers to the scripture verse, Proverbs 18:24, *"A man of many friends comes to ruin, but there is* **a friend who sticks closer than a brother.**" This scripture is obviously referring to a blood-covenant brother, as Dr., Trumbull has just described. Jonathan and David made such a covenant with each other as recorded in I Samuel 18.

"Now it came about that when he had finished speaking to Saul, that the soul of Jonathan was knit to the soul of David, and Jonathan loved him as himself. And Saul took him that day and did not let him return to his father's house. Then Jonathan made a covenant with David because he loved him as himself. And Jonathan stripped himself of the robe that was on him and gave it to David with his armor, including his sword and his bow and his belt" (I Samuel 18:1-4).

These types of understandings still exist in oriental and Middle Eastern cultures today. This is why it is still such a serious matter in many countries for an Arab Muslim to become a Christian. In their way of thinking, the man is in covenant through Islam with Allah and his brothers. In becoming a Christian, according to eastern thinking, a man is breaking this covenant with Allah and his brothers and thus is worthy of death. In many cultures, his own mother is sworn to seek his

[2]Trumbull, H. Clay, *The Blood Covenant*, Kirkwood, Mo. Impact Books, Inc., 1975, pp.5-6

[3]Trumbull, H. Clay, *ibid.* p.7

death. Since covenant is an unconditional, irrevocable, indissoluble commitment breakable only by death, covenant breaking in the East is virtually always punishable by death. When men made such a covenant with each other, they made a commitment to each other more valuable than even their own lives. When entering into such a covenant, they made the basic commitment to each other that "all I have and all I am is yours. Your enemies are my enemies, and I am ready to give up even my life for you, if need be."

It is an astounding thing that Almighty God would make covenant with man, committing all He is and all He has to us. Jesus Christ took upon Himself the punishment for our covenant breaking in His establishment of the New Covenant, and offered to all who will receive an irrevocable, indissoluble covenant commitment.

Covenant Is Not Dependent Upon Performance

The concept of covenant then, is a unilateral, unconditional, irrevocable, commitment before God, valid until death. Covenant does not depend upon the performance of either party. Covenant is a unilateral commitment made to another party in the presence of God and is independent of the performance of the other party.

This means that if a man gave his word in covenant, his fulfillment of that word was not dependent upon whether the other man fulfilled his word or not. It was a unilateral commitment before God. In other words, each man had chosen in advance to live a free life, not dependent upon the choices of others, but rather dependent upon unilateral choices and commitments made before God. Because of this understanding, it was very rare for an eastern man to ever break a covenant. If someone did, the entire society was outraged and all were committed to impose upon the covenant breaker the penalty for such behavior, death. It is amazing to note that in ancient Israel, even when a covenant was entered into with purposeful deceit, the covenant vow was still kept. Even after the deceit was discovered, the honorable men of Israel still fulfilled their covenant vow to a deceitful heathen nation. This story is recorded in the ninth chapter of the book of Joshua.

God had instructed Joshua and the Israelites to eliminate from the land all the Canaanites living there. They had already totally annihilated the cities of Jericho and Ai, and were now nearing the Canaanite city of Gibeon. The Gibeonites had heard what had been done to Jericho and Ai and were greatly frightened. The elders of the city devised a plan to deceive Joshua, and induce him to enter into a covenant of peace with them. They knew that if they could get the Israelites to enter into a covenant with them, Israel would then be bound to do them no harm.

The Gibeonites sent an envoy to the Israelite camp with worn-out shoes and clothing, stale bread, and cracked and mended wineskins to make it appear as if they had traveled a very great distance. They arrived and appeared before Joshua in this condition and sought to enter into a covenant of peace, saying that they were not inhabitants of the land of Canaan, but rather lived a very great distance away. Joshua and the elders of Israel did not seek the counsel of the Lord, but rather believed the Gibeonites and cut a covenant of peace with them. Only three days later, Joshua discovered that the Gibeonites had deceived him and were occupants of the land of Canaan. Although all of Israel would have liked to destroy the Gibeonites, Joshua and the leaders prevented them because of the covenant, which was made with them.

"So the men of Israel took some of their provisions and did not ask for the counsel of the Lord. And Joshua made peace with them and made a covenant with them, to let them live, and the leaders of the congregation swore an oath to them. And it came about at the end of three days after they had made a covenant with them, that they heard that they were neighbors and that they were living within their land. Then the sons of Israel set out and

came to their cities on the third day. Now their cities were Gibeon, and Chephirah and Beeroth and Kiriath-jearim. And the sons of Israel did not strike them because the leaders of the congregation had sworn to them by the Lord, the God of Israel. And the whole congregation grumbled against the leaders. But all the leaders said to the whole congregation, 'We have sworn to them by the Lord, the God of Israel, and now we cannot touch them. Thus we will so do to them, even let them live, lest wrath be on us for the oath which we swore to them'" (Joshua 9:14-19).

Despite the fact that it was a covenant that was never meant to be and even was entered into through fraud and deception, once it was made, the Israelites were bound to honor their word. Joshua and his leaders understood the issue of covenant and its value before God. They could not break their covenant even though it was made in deception with heathen Canaanites whom God had commanded the Israelites to destroy.

Joshua's concept of covenant was so strong that not only did he preserve the Gibeonites, but in Joshua chapter ten, he and the Israelites fought alongside the Gibeonites to help defeat the enemies of their covenant partners. God so honored the value of this covenant that He placed it even above the individual welfare of His chosen people Israel. In II Samuel chapter 21, a famine had been released upon Israel. When King David inquired of the Lord as to the cause of the famine, the Lord informed him that it was a result of King Saul's violation of the covenant by putting the Gibeonites to death. The famine was terminated only as King David went to the Gibeonites and repented and made restitution for the rebellious acts of former King Saul. We see here again the incredible value God places on covenant as He honors and calls Israel to honor a covenant that should have never been made in the first place.

"When you make a vow to God, do not be late in paying it, for He takes no delight in fools. Pay what you vow" (i.e. Annanias & Saphira, Acts 5). *"It is better that you should not vow than that you should vow and not pay. Do not let your speech cause you to sin and do not say in the presence of the messenger of God that it was a mistake. Why should God be*

angry on account of your voice and destroy the work of your hands?" (Ecclesiastes 5:4-6).

Seven Components of a Covenant

Let us now briefly examine the components of a traditional eastern covenant ceremony. The following seven components were usually included:

1. Unilateral commitment before God: The two parties would make a commitment to each other which was unilateral (not dependent upon the fulfillment by the other party), and spoken in the presence of God.

2. Terms expressed: The terms of the covenant were specified, including duration and scope of commitment. Most frequently when men would become blood brothers in covenant with each other, the duration was not only until death of the two covenanting partners, but frequently extended for several generations. God says that His covenant lasts to 1,000 generations (Psalm 106:8-10). David's covenant with Jonathan lasted at least through the next generation, as he sought out and blessed Mephibosheth, Jonathan's son for the sake of covenant with Jonathan (II Samuel 9). Most covenants extend at least until death of the covenanting partners. The scope of the covenant among blood covenant friends would entail a commitment of all available resources up to and including one's own life. "All I have and all I am is yours," was the commitment that was made. This again is the commitment which God makes to us in Christ.

3. Exchange of gifts: Men would traditionally exchange four very valuable gifts as earnest commitment of their sincerity toward God and one another. These four gifts were:

   A. Their coats or robes: The coat signified tribe, standing within the tribe and was representative of tribal

44

and family identity and authority. To give a man your coat was to give him the benefits (inheritance, etc.) and standing which you enjoy in the nation, tribe and family.

B. Their weapon belts: By laying your weapon belt at another man's feet you were saying to him, "I give you all my strength and military might. I will defend you to the death. Any enemy of yours is an enemy of mine. Further more, I will never use these weapons against you. I will not defend myself against you. For I lay myself completely open and defenseless before you."

C. Their names: Men would actually be known from that time forth by at least a part of the other man's name. The name denoted power of attorney. With the power of attorney to use a man's name, you can access his bank account and all his assets. What you say, he will back up. The right to use a man's name was and is very powerful.

D. Blood: Among non-Hebrew peoples then two covenanting friends would usually exchange their own blood in some fashion such as Dr. Trumbull described above. God forbade the Hebrew people from drinking any blood because He did not want them partaking of the very life of another being. He knew that the life of the flesh is in the blood (Leviticus 17:14). Jesus, in John chapter six, spoke of this very thing as He commanded His followers to eat His flesh and drink His blood in order to receive His very life. This, of course, is what we are doing each time we partake of the Lord's Supper.

The Hebrews however did not drink or commingle each other's blood when they made covenant. They more frequently slew an animal and conducted their ceremony using the common blood of animals. This is the methodology we see used as God cut a covenant with Abraham in Genesis chapter 15. The significance of blood being shed is that is indicative of the life of the one cutting covenant. When a man sheds his own blood, or in the case of the Hebrews, the blood of a substitute, he is saying to the other party, "I am willing to give my life for you. I want to unite myself so closely with you that I actually want to be one with you by partaking of the very essence of your being and have your life inside me."

4. Vows: Men would make sacred vows to one another and to God. They would vow fidelity to one another unto death. They frequently would pronounce blessings to be bestowed upon their covenant partner as a result of the covenant and curses upon him should he ever break the covenant. These vows, because they were unilateral vows made unto God, were considered very sacred and were thus never broken.

5. Witnesses: The covenant ceremony was almost always attended by witnesses, who joyfully attested to the making of the covenant. There was frequently appointed a covenant attorney whose job it was to see that the covenant was carried out. Unlike our system of contract today in which each party engages an attorney to protect his interests, under a covenant, there is only one attorney who is not for either party, but rather was a witness of the covenant and was only for the covenant. It was his job to see to it that the vows and terms of the covenant were carried out.

6. Exchange of phylacteries: A phylactery is another word for a token of the covenant. Many times when men would cut a vein in the arm or leg and exchange blood, they would then pour gun powder or some such substance into the wound so as to create a noticeable black

mark or scar which would serve to identify them as a covenant man. Sometimes a copy of the document recording the covenant was worn in some sort of container by both parties on the arm, forehead or around the neck as an amulet. The phylactery was a sign to all that this person had entered into a blood covenant with another party. This is what God instructed the Hebrew people to do when He made a covenant with them through Moses (Exodus 13:16).

7. Sharing of a covenant meal: After men would make a covenant together, as a symbol of their friendship, they would then sit and break bread together in hospitality and friendship.

The reason I have spent the time here to look at these components of a covenant is because most of us as westerners are not familiar with these things because they are no longer a regular part of our culture. However, the entire Bible is a book of covenants. It is not a history book or storybook. It is a book of covenants. It is interesting to me to note that even though most people do not understand covenant in the West at this time, our wedding ceremonies are still structured for the most part as though a marriage were a covenant. Obviously, the men who wrote the traditional wedding ceremony, still used in many contemporary churches, viewed marriage as a covenant. Let's look at the traditional wedding ceremony.

All the components of a blood covenant are inherent in the wedding ceremony.

1. The ceremony is conducted in the presence of God and unilateral promises are usually made to Him. The ceremony opens with words such as, "We are gathered here today in the presence of God and these witnesses to unite this man and this woman in Holy Matrimony, which is an honourable estate, instituted by God signi-

fying unto us the mystical union that is between Christ and His Church."

2. Terms are then expressed such as, "I take thee for better or for worse, for richer or for poorer, in sickness and in health, until death us do part." This again is a unilateral commitment before God of one partner to the other in whatever circumstance may arise until he dies.

3. An exchange of gifts usually does occur. Hopefully the conveyance of the coat signifying standing and worth in each other's family is conveyed. Weapons are not usually conveyed, but hopefully each one makes himself open and vulnerable before the other. The groom usually does give the bride his name. Usually they do not exchange their own blood, however in many Christian churches, the marriage is sealed in communion by the substitutionary blood of Christ, which was shed for both parties. Another symbol of the shedding of blood is the sexual union, which usually occurs on the wedding night. This is another way of becoming one flesh, which is the purpose of the commingling of blood in a heathen blood covenant ceremony. The sexual being is meant to be a way of saying to the covenant partner, "I give you all that I am and all that I have and I allow you access to the most precious and holy aspects of my being."

4. Vows are then pronounced in the ceremony. These vows are again quite unilateral and unconditional in most cases, such as "I take thee to be my lawfully wedded Wife/Husband to have and to hold from this day forward, for better or for worse, for richer or for poorer, in sickness and in health, to love and to cherish, until death do us part, according to God's holy ordinance, and thereto I pledge thee my troth."

5. Witnesses are also present who usually sign a marriage certificate. As a matter of fact, God Himself says that He

is witness at a marriage. *"Because the Lord has been a witness between you and the wife of your youth, against which you have dealt treacherously, though she is your companion and your wife by covenant"* (Malachi 2:14).

6. Phylacteries are then exchanged in the form of rings. These are received and then worn as an outward sign visible to all that this man or woman is in covenant.

7. A covenant meal is oftentimes held at the reception. The wedding cake is actually symbolic of the covenant meal and many times the bride and groom serve this cake to each other in a special way to symbolize their unity and commitment to one another.

Covenant vs. Contract

A covenant is a unilateral, irrevocable, indissoluble commitment before God and valid until death or even into succeeding generations. A covenant is not dependent upon the choices of another, but is a commitment unto death before God.

Let's now contrast this with the concept of a contract. The concept of contract is an entirely different concept. A contract is a bilateral agreement between two parties totally dependent upon performance of the agreement, and breakable by either party upon non-performance of the other. Under a contract, if one party fails to perform according to the contract, the other party has no obligation to perform either and is no longer bound by the terms of the contract. The following chart illustrates the contrast.

Covenant	Contract
Unilateral	Bilateral
Unconditional	Conditional
Irrevocable	Revocable
Indissoluble	Dissoluble

A covenant is based upon the **WORD** of the one making the covenant, while a contract is based upon the **PERFORMANCE (WORKS)** of the other party making the contract. The best word we have in English that means a covenant is a promise. A promise is based on the word of the one making the promise. If the promise maker is a person of integrity, then that promise will be kept regardless of the circumstances.

A covenant says, "I will keep my word and do what I said, whether you do or not." A contract says, "If you keep your part of the agreement, I will keep my part of the agreement. However, if you fail to keep your word, I am released and no longer obligated to keep my word."

Gift vs. Sale

Let me further illustrate this point with an example regarding a car. Suppose that I make an agreement to sell Joe my car for $10,000. Joe has the money and wants the car, and I have the car and want the money. We make a contract to exchange Joe's money for my car.

Now suppose Joe only pays me $5,000, am I obligated to give him the car? Of course not! The reason I am not is that Joe did not fulfill his end of the agreement. He didn't give me the full amount of money that he promised. On the other hand, if Joe gives me the full $10,000 what if I want to keep the money and the car? Can I do this? No! If he gives me the money I must give him the car. Virtually any judge in any country will uphold such an agreement. So if Joe keeps his word, I must keep mine. However, if Joe does not keep his word and fulfill his end of the agreement, then I am released from fulfilling my end of the agreement. This is a contract.

A covenant, on the other hand, is a promise that is independent of the actions of the other party. Suppose instead that I tell Joe, "Joe, because I love you like my own brother, I want to give you my car as a gift. I will make arrangements next week to have my car sent to you. I hereby promise you my car as a gift." Now, what must Joe do to receive the car? Nothing. Simply say, "Thank you."

Now suppose in the ensuing time, Joe becomes offended with me for some other reason and begins telling people lies about me. Suppose he is calling many of my acquaintances and telling them that he knows for certain that I am a drug dealer and adulterer. Another friend advises me of this situation and I am shocked and hurt. Suppose I then call Joe and ask him about this and find that he is indeed offended and has no intention of ceasing his lies about me.

When confronted Joe refuses to change. The question now is, do I still have to send him my car? Joe is not treating me as a friend, why should I send him my car? The answer is: **I must send him my car because I gave him my word**, and if I am a person of integrity, I will fulfill my word because I made Joe a promise. My word is my word independent of any choices, actions or attitudes that Joe might have. I will fulfill my word and keep my promise whether Joe does or not and independent of any way in which Joe treats me. This is a covenant.

Perhaps you can see already that much of our society has lost the meaning of covenant, or the value of a promise, or the integrity of a person's word. This is not just in the arena of marriage, but in many areas of life. Words have become meaningless and unreliable. This is highly unfortunate because basic trust is rooted in the integrity of a person's word. I'm sure that each of us can think of many people around us who have let us down by not honoring their word to us. However, it really is indicative of flea thinking to focus on all the other people who have dishonored their word. The free man looks to see if he is truly a person of integrity who keeps his word, or in what areas has he been one who has let his word be dependent upon circumstances or the choices of other people.

Collision Course

Two battleships assigned to the training squadron had been at sea on maneuvers in heavy weather for several days. I was serving on the lead battleship and was on watch on the bridge as night fell. The visibility was poor with patchy fog, so the captain remained on the bridge keeping an eye on all activities.

Shortly after dark, the lookout on the wing of the bridge reported, "Light, bearing on the starboard bow."

"Is it steady or moving astern?" the captain called out.

Lookout replied, "Steady, captain," which meant we were on a dangerous collision course with that ship.

The captain then called to the signalman, "Signal that ship, 'We are on a collision course, advise you change course 20 degrees.'"

Back came a signal, "Advisable for you to change course 20 degrees."

The captain said, "Send, I'm a captain, change course 20 degrees."

"I'm a seaman second class," came the reply. "You had better change course 20 degrees."

By that time, the captain was furious. He spat out, "Send, I'm a battleship. Change course 20 degrees."

Back came the flashing light, "I'm a lighthouse."

We changed course.

The paradigm shift experienced by the captain — and by us as we read this account — puts the situation in a totally different light. We can see a reality that is superseded by his limited perception — a reality that is critical for us to understand in our daily lives as it was for the captain in the fog.

Principles are like lighthouses. They are natural laws that cannot be broken. As Cecil B. deMille observed of the principles contained in his monumental movie, The Ten Commandments, *"It is impossible for us to break the law. We can only break ourselves against the law."*

While individuals may look at their own lives and interactions in terms of paradigms or maps emerging out of their experience and conditioning, these maps are not the territory. They are "subjective reality," only an attempt to describe the territory.

The "objective reality," or the territory itself, is composed of "lighthouse" principles that govern human growth and happiness — natural laws that are woven into the fabric of every civilized society throughout history and comprise the roots of every family and institution that has endured and prospered. The degree to which our mental maps accurately describe the territory does not alter its existence.[4]

These observations made by Steven Covey regarding the above story are profound. It is indeed true that principles are like lighthouses. They will not move, no matter how big our ship is, how many people are on board our ship, or how long we have been driving our ship toward the lighthouse. It doesn't matter whether our map shows rocks and a lighthouse ahead or not. If there truly is a lighthouse and there are rocks dead ahead, even if our map shows only open sea and no rocks, at some point we need to wake up and realize that our map (paradigms, values, beliefs) is wrong and does not line up with the actual lay of the land and sea (principles). Remains of other ships ahead of us wrecked on the rocks might be a strong clue that our map is faulty.

---

[4] Covey, Steven, *The Seven Habits of Highly Effective People*, New York, NY, Simon and Schuster 1989, p. 33

Societal Consequences of Value Exchange

The fact that marriage was designed by God to be a covenant, rather than a contract, is one of those lighthouse principles. In our western society, we have thought that the value of marriage as a covenant was a ship coming towards us that we could simply command to change course so that we could continue on the course of embracing marriage as a contract. However, the fact that God designed marriage as a covenant is a lighthouse principle, not another ship that can be turned out of our way. Unfortunately, the result is that we are driving our ship onto the rocks, all the while continuing to curse the lighthouse for not moving out of our way. We, as a society, have continued to believe that our map (value of marriage as a contract) is correct even in the face of an ever-increasing number of ships crashing on the rocks in front of us. Below is evidence that maybe our map has not given us correct information.

"Marriage is also the bedrock of stable families, strong communities and a healthy society...

Now 30 years into the experiment with easy divorce, we're seeing that we the earlier consensus was right. As far as children's well-being goes, divorce is a calamity. According to 'Father Facts,' a publication of the National Fatherhood Initiative, children of divorce are much more likely to drop out of school, to engage in premarital sex, and to become pregnant than children of intact families. The average income of women with children declines by 73% after divorce. The advantage of growing up with educated parents is obliterated by divorce.

Only 8.3% of children living with both parents exhibit significant emotional or behavioral problems, compared with 19.1% of those living with their mothers only, and 23.6% of those living with their mothers and stepfathers."[5]

---

[5] Charen, Mona, *Divorce Reform Puts Families First*, Rocky Mountain News, Denver, CO, February 15, 1996

These above statistics are from some time past now. However, in the last decade, the divorce rate, and the incidence of serious problems in the lives of children of divorce in the US and most other western countries has not declined, but rather has still increased even more. When a society embraces practices based on values that do not line up with true principles, that society will naturally self-destruct.

Unfortunately, we have experienced a major value exchange over the last fifty years or so of covenant for contract in marriage. Most people in the 1950s would have held a value that marriage is a covenant. I would suspect that most people today in western society would hold a value that marriage is a contract. However, we still use covenant language and pretend as though we think it is a covenant at wedding ceremonies.

I believe that in marriage this exchange of the value of covenant for the value of contract is responsible for a major portion of the abuse and dysfunction currently taking place in families. The covenant value in marriage would say to the marriage partner, "I am irrevocably committed to you until death separates us. My commitment to you has nothing to do with your performance or any choice you make. It is a unilateral commitment before God unto death." This is the commitment that Jesus has made to us. *"I will never leave you or forsake you"* (Hebrews 13:5).

The contract value would rather say, "I'll keep my end of the bargain if you keep yours. If you make me unhappy or don't do what you promised, then I will leave you and find someone else who makes me happy and keeps his promises. And if you leave me, then I will definitely leave you and find someone else."

The result of this value exchange in my opinion has been devastating to the state of the family and of society. We now have a generation of people growing up who have no sense of permanency in anything. Everything is temporary and there is no stability to life. You tell such people that God is stable and that His word says that He never changes and yet they cannot believe it. We have a generation of youth who cannot commit to anything. They have no ability to think long term, so they simply make devastating short-sighted choices for themselves and their families as they marry, or simply cohabit without marriage.

We have taken those things, which are meant to be holy and desecrated them, making them common, and thereby stripped them of their value. Only that which is rare and special has value. That which is common is ordinary and carries no value. Covenant commitment is meant to protect the heart from damage. As we have forsaken the value of covenant in marriage, many have exposed the hearts of our youth to pressures and pain that God never intended for anyone's heart to experience. Because of this pain and deep wounding, pain avoidance has become the major value and the driving force of many peoples' lives.

> We now have a generation of people growing up who have no sense of permanency in anything.

If the Salt Is Not Salty

Even more unfortunate is the fact that the vast majority of the church in western nations has embraced the same contract value regarding marriage as the society around it. Speaking of believers, Jesus said, *"You are the salt of the earth; when the salt loses its flavor, how shall it be seasoned. It is then good for nothing but to be thrown out and trampled underfoot by men"* (Matthew 5:13).

The purpose of salt is to season and preserve. If the salt has become the same as the food it should season or preserve, it no longer seasons or preserves and it has lost its purpose and mission. I am told that in most western nations, the divorce rate among those who attend church is equal to, or in some cases higher than that of those who are not a part of the church. It would thus appear, that in the arena of marriage, the church has lost its saltiness. I believe that now is the time for this to be restored.

Divorce was a very uncommon and tragic event during the years in which I grew up. I remember hearing news of a particular classmate of mine in seventh grade whose parents were divorcing. This was big news in our school of 1200 students, as it was so uncommon. You may think that I attended a private Christian school or lived in an isolated rural town. No, I attended a public school in a major metropolitan city (Denver, Colorado), and still news of a seventh grade student whose parents were divorcing was big news in 1967. By the time my children were in elementary school, two and a half decades later, there were only a couple of students in the class still living with both original married parents. Divorce had become so common that it was considered normal in the class for most children's parents to have experienced a divorce.

How has this value exchange of covenant for contract taken place in our society? If we were to supernaturally transport a Christian from the 1950s into our present culture, he would probably be shocked at the values that are currently accepted in the church as opposed to those accepted in the 1950s culture. This shift in values has not happened overnight, but rather over a significant period of time.

The Frog In The Kettle

I believe that the value exchanges that we have experienced are not random, but rather are the result of strategies purposefully executed by the kingdom of darkness. The primary strategy that has been employed to change this value is to make the change slowly enough that no one really notices. This is similar to the strategy of boiling a frog in a kettle by slowly turning up the heat.

I am told (I have never tried it, and thus no frogs were harmed in the writing of this book) that a frog can be boiled alive and never sense the danger if the heat in the kettle is turned up slowly enough. Since a frog is a cold-blooded animal, it simply changes its body temperature to match its surrounding environment. If you toss a frog into a pot of boiling water, it will immediately sense the large difference between its current body temperature and the temperature of the water, recognize danger and jump out of the kettle.

However, if you toss a frog into a kettle of room-temperature water, it will be very happy and remain in the pot. The temperature may then be turned up a couple of degrees per hour. Each time the temperature is changed, since the incremental difference is small, the frog simply adjusts its body temperature to match the surrounding water, not recognizing any danger. I am told that if one continues this process over a couple of days, the temperature can be slowly turned up to the point of boiling, and the frog will never sense the danger and thus will actually remain in the kettle as it is slowly boiled to death.

I believe that this is the strategy that the kingdom of darkness has utilized in changing values within the church and society. A person from the 1950s transposed into our current culture would immediately sense a very large divergence in values and immediately sense danger. However, if values are changed slowly over a period of several decades, most people simply change their personal values a very small amount each year, never realizing the change that has taken place over forty or fifty years. We then come to accept things today as normal that fifty or sixty years ago we would have totally rejected as unacceptable.

The consequence of this value exchange in marriage is that we have made it increasingly more difficult for each succeeding generating to experience a successful marriage and family. When the value of covenant is not in place within a marriage, it becomes very difficult to be honest, open and transparent before each other. Because the heart is very sensitive, much like the raw nerve I described in the beginning of this chapter, if it is exposed outside of the protective tooth enamel of covenant, it may experience excruciating pain and may not survive.

When the protective tooth enamel of covenant is not in place around a couple, then each person begins to create his own protective hardened shell around his own heart. There is a continual fear that if I do not measure up to the expectations of my spouse he will abandon me. "If I have made a serious mistake or have done something that will hurt or anger my spouse, he might leave me." This type of fear is prevalent when the protective hedge of covenant is not in place in a marriage. It causes people to hide and keep secrets from each other. A protective shell then grows up between the couple rather than around them. Fleas will always work to protect themselves and their own interests at the expense of others. This is why the first step in moving your marriage from fleadom to freedom is to deal with the fear in your own heart, tear down the protective wall between you and your spouse, and establish a personal commitment to covenant in your own marriage.

The critical value question, which you need to answer for yourself is this: **Is your marriage a covenant before God or is it a contract?** To what did you commit on your wedding day? Did you commit before God and witnesses to your spouse "until death us do part?" What words (vows) did you actually speak? Are you a reactive flea controlled by the words and behavior of your spouse and others, or are you a free person, able to choose to honor a commitment to God and your spouse, whether he does or not?

Reflection

1. Covenant in marriage protects the heart like tooth enamel protects the nerve.

2. Covenant in marriage is a unilateral, unconditional, irrevocable promise, breakable only by death.

3. My choice to keep my covenant word is not dependent upon the choices, attitudes or behavior of my spouse.

4. Our traditional wedding ceremony contains all 7 of the components of an eastern blood covenant.

    a. Unilateral promise made before God.

    b. Terms expressed: Until death us do part.

    c. Exchange of gifts.

    d. Vows pronounced.

    e. Witnesses present.

    f. Exchange of tokens: rings.

    g. Sharing of a covenant meal.

5. Covenant is a totally different concept from a contract:

Covenant	Contract
Unilateral	Bilateral
Unconditional	Conditional
Irrevocable	Revocable
Indissoluble	Dissoluble

6. A covenant is based upon the word and integrity of the covenant maker, while a contract is based upon the works and performance of the other party to the contract.

7. In our society, we have exchanged the value of covenant for the value of contract in marriage and are mistaking the lighthouse for another ship.

8. We are making it difficult for our children and future generations to prosper in marriage by embracing the value exchange of covenant for contract in marriage in our generation.

9. This value exchange has happened slowly over time, like boiling a frog in a kettle.

10. Have you recognized that up until now you have actually considered your marriage more of a contract than a covenant? Are you now willing to personally recommit yourself and your marriage to covenant?

Resources

☐1☐ *An Ancient Paths Seminar:* Covenant Marriage (Covenant Marriage Retreat). See Appendix for details and www.familyfoundations.com for schedule of upcoming events.

🎧 The Blood Covenant 1 and 2

🎧 Covenant Strength at the City Wall

🎧 The Power of Covenant in Marriage

c h a p t e r   4

Power of the
Threshold
Covenant

I n understanding the power of establishing the protective
hedge of covenant around our marriage again, it is very helpful
for us as westerners to gain more insight into the eastern
understanding of the concept of covenant. There is a particularly
beautiful understanding of covenant that is depicted in eastern
culture and described by Dr. H. Clay Trumbull in his very
enlightening book, *The Threshold Covenant.*[1] The relationship
described between an eastern host and guest when entering into
a "threshold covenant" is worth taking a chapter in this book to
describe just to help us as westerners obtain an understanding of
the power of covenant protection that can be applied to our
marriage. Most of the understanding of the threshold covenant

---

[1] Trumbull, H. Clay, *The Threshold Covenant*, Edinburgh, T. & T. Clark,
1896

described in this chapter has come from the research put forth in Dr. Trumbull's book, *The Threshold Covenant.*[2]

I have found that there are several profound concepts and principles in the Bible that we, as westerners, totally miss simply because the eastern imagery is unfamiliar to us. This image of the covenant of hospitality extended by a host to a guest is one of those concepts that has been totally misunderstood in most western culture and thus vital biblical principles have been totally missed or even wrongly interpreted.

The concept of the threshold covenant has to do with the relationship between a guest and host as the guest crosses the threshold of the host's dwelling. There is an implied covenant of hospitality into which both parties enter upon the entrance of the guest into the dwelling of the host.

I have personally observed that eastern people have a much stronger concept of hospitality than do we in the West. As I have traveled in the Middle East, I have stayed with various Middle Eastern families. I remember on one of my first trips admiring a painting on the wall of the home in which we were staying. The next day, much to my dismay, I found that very painting removed from the wall, wrapped in paper and delivered to me as a gift. I did not mean for the host to give me the painting, I was merely admiring it. I have never had this happen to me in a western home.

In the West we use such phrases as, "Make yourself at home," or, "Mi casa—su casa" ("my house is your house"), but we don't really mean it! In the East, they mean it. "Whatever I have, if it is of benefit to you, it is yours." This type of hospitality is really a foreign concept to most of us who have grown up in North America or European-based cultures.

---

[2] Trumbull, H. Clay, *ibid.*

Getting back to the threshold greeting custom, it may be described as follows. When a host is aware that a guest is coming to call upon him, the host will greet the guest with an offering of blood poured out at the threshold of the host's dwelling.

Covenants in the East have for centuries been ratified by the outpouring of blood. In the western mind, blood is usually thought of as representing death. When we see blood, we think of death. In the eastern mindset, however, blood is usually thought to represent life. God told the Hebrew people in Leviticus 17:11 *"For the life of the flesh is in the blood, and I have given it to you upon the altar to make atonement for your souls; for it is the blood that makes atonement for the soul."* So the blood poured out at the threshold was representative of the life of the host.

The outpouring of this blood sacrifice serves then as an invitation to the guest that the host is willing to receive, in peace, him as a guest. The more honor the host wishes to convey to the guest, the more costly is the blood poured out. If the guest is someone not highly esteemed, the blood of a dove or pigeon might be offered. If he is someone more esteemed, then perhaps the blood of a goat or an oxen. If the guest is a king, then the blood of a very special animal called "the fatted calf" reserved only for a king is poured out.

This greeting custom was, and still is in some parts of the Middle East today, commonly known and practiced. The duty of the host is to pour out the sacrifice of blood at the threshold of his dwelling. The duty then of the guest, upon observing the blood poured out, thus indicating an invitation to enter the dwelling as a guest, is to step across the blood and the threshold and into covenant with the host.

You may have seen a few years back the movie, *Not Without My Daughter*.[3] If so, you may remember a scene in the movie (this

---

[3] *Not Without My Daughter*, Hollywood, CA, Metro-Goldwyn-Mayer, 1990

scene is sometimes edited out on television versions) when the Iranian man with his American wife first arrived at his family's home in Iran. They were greeted by the family, and a goat had been slain in front of the house as a welcome to them. The little girl was screaming at the sight of the blood, and the American wife didn't know what to make of this, but the Iranian husband told them, not to worry, that it was just a greeting custom welcoming them and they just needed to step over the bloody animal and enter into the house. So we see that even as recently as the 1980s such a custom of pouring out the blood of an animal was still common practice in certain homes in the Middle East.

Don't Step On the Threshold

The greatest insult to be proffered by the guest would be to step on the threshold and in the blood poured out by the host. Since the blood represented the life of the host, to step in the blood was to put under ones feet the life of the host. Offering a blood sacrifice would be the equivalent in the West of extending ones hand in friendship as a greeting. To step in the blood on the threshold would be tantamount in the West to refusing to shake the host's hand and instead spitting in his face.

If you step in the blood, you are refusing the offer of hospitality, and are insulting the host. You had better have brought your army with you as this would be a declaration of war against the host. This is the very imagery used in Hebrews 10:29 regarding trampling underfoot the blood of the covenant. Without understanding the concept of the threshold covenant, this scripture makes very little sense. The author of Hebrews tells us that to go on sinning willfully after receiving knowledge of the truth is a covenant violation. *"Or how much worse punishment do you suppose will he be thought worthy who has trampled the Son of God underfoot, counted the blood of the covenant by which he was sanctified a common thing and insulted the Spirit of grace?"* (Hebrews 10:29).

It is common knowledge in the East that one does not step on the threshold of a dwelling, but always over the threshold. Superstitions have grown up around this even in the West, advising people not to step even on cracks, but rather over them. Perhaps you have heard, "Step on a crack, break your mother's back." Such a phrase originally comes from the concept of stepping over the threshold and not on it.

We also still have another practice that stems from this concept of stepping over the threshold and entering into a binding covenant. I am told that in ancient times when a couple was married, it was common practice for the groom to build a home for himself and his bride to live in. When the home was completed, he would then come for his bride and take her to the home he had built. The groom would then have poured out the most costly blood offering available to him upon the threshold of the dwelling. Upon approaching the home, he would then pick his bride up in his arms and carry her across the blood and the threshold and into their new life together. Tradition says that when his right foot hit the inside of the dwelling with his bride in his arms, she was at that moment forever bonded into the groom's family and was a part of the family from that time forth. On the wedding night, a groom still carries his bride over the threshold today, but no one can tell you why.

Another aspect of this implied threshold covenant was that no honorable man would step over the threshold of a man's dwelling with the intent of doing the host harm. If a thief intended to steal from a man, he would never enter the home through the front door. If he did so, he would make himself a covenant breaker and thus curse his life with God. Consequently, a thief would enter through a window or some other entrance, but never across the threshold of the front door. Jesus used this very imagery in John 10:1 when he said that he who enters the sheepfold some other way than the front door is a thief and a robber. This of course was very familiar to His listeners of that time but not familiar to most of us today.

Another custom from ancient culture depicting this under-standing of the covenant of hospitality established when crossing a threshold has to do with the way a conquering general would enter a conquered city. I am told that it was also common cus-tom for a conquering general to enter the conquered city through a breach in the city wall or through some entrance other than the main gate. By so doing, he was signifying that he was coming as a conqueror and not as a guest, and was not willing to submit himself to the authority of the city. Had he entered through the main gate and stepped across the threshold of the city, he would then be signifying that he enters as a guest subject to the covenant of hospitality. By entering through a breach in the wall or through some alternative entrance the general was making a statement, "I do not bow to your authority, but rather I come as a conqueror. I come to establish a new authority to which you must bow, not to submit to your authority."

A Greek Olympian in later times was granted the right to enter the city through a small breach in the wall, rather than through the front gate. In so doing, the Olympian was being treated as a conqueror, rather than as a citizen of the city, and thus afforded rights and privileges above the common citizenry of the city.[4]

So, we understand that when an invited guest crossed the threshold of the host's home he was agreeing to come in and abide under the authority of the host and to submit to that host while in his home. The guest is obligated to support, honor and bless the host while in his home. The host, on the other hand, by receiving the guest is obligated to provide for and protect the guest while he is in his home. How strong is this covenant of hospitality? So strong that a host would even protect a stranger who is in his home as a guest with his own life.

---

[4] Trumbull, H. Clay, *ibid.* pp. 6-7

Abiding Under the Shadow

Let's look at a biblical example of this type of protection afforded a guest who has entered into this covenant of hospitality. The story of Lot and his family giving refuge to two angels is recorded in Genesis 19. In Lot's time, there were not many inns available in which travelers could stay. So, it was common practice that residents of a city would invite travelers to stay the night with them. In this case, two angels have been sent by the Lord to warn Lot of the impending doom of the city. Lot, however, does not yet recognize that these men are angels and supposes them only to be human travelers. He then offers them accommodation and hospitality in his home for the night.

The wicked men of the city then come to Lot's home and demand that he grant them access to the two strangers that they might homosexually rape them. Lot's response is as follows:

"So Lot went out to them through the doorway, shut the door behind him and said, 'Please my brethren, do not do so wickedly! See now, I have two daughters who have not known a man; please let me bring them out to you and you may do to them as you wish; only do nothing to these men, **since this is the reason they have come under the shadow of my roof"** (Genesis 19:6-8).

Most of us as westerners are quite shocked when we read this account. We are initially shocked at the fact that Lot would protect strangers with his own life and the lives of his daughters. This again has to do with a covenant mentality. When the two men step across the threshold of Lot's home, they have entered into an implied covenant of hospitality whereby they agree to submit to Lot's authority and he agrees to protect them, provide for them, and treat them as though they were a part of his own family.

When Lot tells the men of the city that he would rather let them ravage his own virgin daughters than to harm the men who are his guests, again we are quite shocked. In understanding the Hebrew mindset here, I believe that Lot is not actually offering to send out his virgin daughters to be raped and ravaged by this lust-filled perverted crowd. He is saying to them something like the following. "Because I am an honorable man, and these two strangers have entered into my home as guests, I am willing to protect them with my life. I will uphold my covenant of hospitality with them. You would have to kill me, and my whole family before I will allow any harm to come to my guests. Do you understand the degree to which a father loves and is willing to protect his own daughter? (Every father understands this.) Well, I am telling you that I would rather allow you to attack and rape my virgin daughters before I will allow you to harm these two guests. And I would protect my daughters with every available resource including my own life. That's the degree to which I will uphold the covenant and protect my guests." So Lot is not actually offering his daughters to the wicked men. He is just letting them know to what extreme extent he will go to protect his guests.

Another very interesting Hebrew idiom is used in this passage. Lot states that the reason he will protect the guests is that "they have come **under the shadow** of my roof." I am told that this phrase, "under the shadow of my roof" is a Hebrew idiom denoting a covenant commitment unto death. If I have come under the shadow of someone's roof, that means that I have entered into threshold covenant with that host and that I agree to abide under his authority as one of his own family members and that he agrees to provide for me and protect me unto death, utilizing all resources available to him including his own life. In this prior passage we see Lot doing exactly this.

Entering into a threshold covenant could be very advantageous depending upon the authority, influence and resource base of the one with whom you were covenanting. To cross the threshold of the tent of an indigent person may not be of great benefit. However, to cross the threshold of the palace of the king of a nation would be significantly more beneficial. Each of these persons may agree to provide for you and protect you with their entire resource base. Obviously it would be much more advantageous to enter into covenant with the one who has great resources than with the one who has little to no resources with which to provide for you or protect you.

Once understanding the threshold covenant and this Hebrew idiom mentioned above, we are now prepared to really understand what the Psalmist is pointing out in Psalm 91. In this Psalm the same Hebrew idiom **"under the shadow of my roof"** is used. However, most of us casually read over it with no understanding of its incredible significance in light of threshold covenant.

"He who dwells in the secret place of the Most High, shall abide under the shadow of the Almighty. I will say of the Lord, He is my refuge and my fortress; My God, in Him will I trust" (Psalm 91:1-2).

In this passage, God Almighty is telling us that when we step across the threshold of His eternal dwelling and come into covenant with Him, He will provide for us and protect us with all of the resources available to Him. This is an incredible statement, that if truly understood, should eliminate, for any person who has entered into this covenant with God, any fear of being harmed or killed.

Saved By Threshold Covenant

This very principle was dramatically made real to me several years ago through an experience shared with me by a Palestinian Arab man whose life had been spared as a result of an implied threshold covenant. Abed (not his real name) as a young man had owned a rather old automobile, which he used for transportation in the Middle Eastern city in which he was living. One day while driving about the city, the brakes went out on his car. Desperately trying to keep his car under control and bring it to a stop, he found himself weaving in and out of pedestrians in the street. Unfortunately, Abed was not able to dodge a young teenage boy walking in the street and mowed him down with his car. After he brought the car to a stop, he ran back to see what had happened to the boy. The injuries of this young teen seemed to be quite serious. Fortunately, Abed was able to flag down another motorist into whose vehicle they quickly loaded the young man and rushed him to a nearby hospital.

After getting the injured pedestrian into the care of the doctors in the hospital, Abed went out of the hospital, and as would have been common custom in that city at that time, knocked on the door of a nearby house seeking a place to recover from the trauma. The nearby house was owned by a young couple who invited Abed in to rest and collect himself. While he was in the bathroom washing the young man's blood off of his hands and clothing, the father of the young woman in whose house Abed had taken refuge came running excitedly into the house yelling for his son-in-law.

This father excitedly explained to his son-in-law that his youngest son, his daughter's youngest brother had just been hit in the street by some crazy motorist and was even now in the hospital next door fighting for his life with several broken bones and internal injuries. He exclaimed to his son-in-law, "Come quickly and help me hunt down this motorist and kill him to avenge what he has done to my son, your brother-in-law." As the son-in-law was readying himself to go help hunt down and kill the motorist, Abed emerged from the bathroom. The father inquired, "Who are you?" As Abed began to explain the trauma he had just been through, everyone suddenly realized that Abed was the very motorist they were going to look for.

The father pulled out a knife and lunged toward Abed, intent on killing him. However, his own son-in-law intervened, staying his father-in-law's hand and stepping in between the two parties. The father-in-law angrily screamed, "Let me go. He must die! He must die!" The son-in-law then very forcefully repelled the father backward and told him, "I agree with you that this man deserves to die for his careless actions and the harm he has done to your son. However, he has stepped across the threshold and is a guest in my home. Father, you know the honor that must be conveyed to a guest. As long as Abed is in my home, I will protect him with my own life, even against you, and you shall do him no harm. Now, as soon as he leaves my home, I will help you kill him in the street."

Abed told me that he decided to continue to remain in the home for some time. After a couple of hours passed, tempers cooled down, and news came from the hospital that young man would live, and that there would be no permanent damage from the accident. Abed was then able to secure the forgiveness of the father and family and was able to leave the home in peace.

As Abed shared this story with me, I was greatly impressed by the degree to which the threshold covenant was honored in his Arab culture. It was incredible to me that this young house-holder was willing to oppose his own father-in-law on behalf of a stranger with whom he had entered into an implied threshold covenant.

In the West, we have a phrase, "blood is thicker than water," usually meaning that a family relationship of people who are blood relatives will supersede any other type of relationship including that of friendship, trade, etc. However, I'm told that in the East, the common phrase is "blood is thicker than milk." This saying implies that two men who have entered into a blood covenant will have a stronger bond than two brothers who have drunk milk from the same mother's breast.

I believe that this threshold covenant is meant to picture the covenant commitment designed to be upheld in marriage. You can readily see that this understanding that my friend Abed and his Arab culture had of covenant does not lend itself to a flea mentality. A flea would certainly not be willing to protect a threshold covenant guest at the expense of self and family. A flea would always put meeting the needs of self above honoring the covenant made with a guest. Only a free man is able to honor a covenant commitment when it is not convenient or may even be dangerous, or very costly to do so. Again, a flea is not free to make a choice based upon values that transcend immediate personal fulfillment. My friend Abed's life was spared by the fact that the young householder's covenant commitment to his guest was based on the integrity of his implied word even when the circumstances drastically changed and it became potentially very costly for him to honor his covenant of hospitality with his guest.

In order for there to be a protective hedge around a marriage, such as the tooth enamel I described that was meant to protect young Don's raw nerve, there must be in place around that marriage a covenant commitment at least as strong as the threshold covenant that I have just described.

> In order for there to be a protective hedge around a marriage, there must be in place a covenant commitment at least as strong as the threshold covenant

As the threshold covenant is applied to marriage, the groom would be pictured as the host receiving his bride as an honored guest into his home and family. To the degree to which Lot and Abed's young householder were willing to fight to the death against even family members on behalf of the guest, this is the degree to which a husband is meant to provide for, protect, and fight for his wife.

The bride's obligation then is to step across the threshold into the groom's house with a willingness to respect her husband and to receive his provision and protection, and to abide under his authority.

In light of this, you may want to consider whether you have committed your marriage relationship to covenant, or you are still operating out of a contract mentality. It is certain that the consideration of the decision to commit yourself to a true covenant lifestyle in your marriage will stir up within you your own flea nature. The flea nature will never commit to covenant in any relationship. Covenant entails protecting and meeting the needs of another at one's own expense. Remember, the nature of a flea is to meet the immediate needs of self above all else. So, a flea will never consider enduring inconvenience, pain, suffering or death for the sake of the one with whom he is in relationship.

Only a truly free man or woman, plugged into the life and power of God, acting as a battery, rather than a flea, is able to walk in covenant with a spouse. Let the fears stirred up in you (what about me?) by making a covenant commitment to your spouse be an indicator to you of areas to look to the Lord rather than to your spouse for life.

Thus, a key step in moving your marriage from fleadom to freedom is to make a decision to embrace the value of covenant in your marriage. Make a decision that you will honor your word (marriage vows) independent of anything your spouse ever does or says. Determine in your heart that regarding your marriage covenant, from this day forward you will act as a free person rather than a flea. This will entail looking to God to meet the needs and desires that your spouse is not currently meeting.

Understanding the Passover

I would now like to examine a couple other aspects of the threshold covenant. In ancient times, it was common practice for a King to travel throughout his land securing the loyalty of his subjects and ridding the land of his enemies. Especially as new land was conquered, the King would travel throughout the newly conquered territory declaring the terms of his kingdom, the duties, obligations, and privileges (i.e. taxes, army conscription, protection) of citizenship.

As mentioned earlier, the common greeting custom in the Ancient East was to pour out blood at the threshold of the dwelling thereby inviting the guest to enter into covenant friendship. Most people raised and reserved one particular animal called "the fatted calf," in the event that the king would ever come to that village. It was a great honor, but not a common occurrence, that the king might visit your particular home in your particular village.

So, if news went out that the king was coming to your village, you would slay the fatted calf, prepare a feast, and prepare to pour out its blood at your dwelling threshold in hopes that the king would choose your house to personally visit. A feast with "the fatted calf" was not prepared for anyone but the king.

This eastern picture helps us to understand what great honor the father in Jesus' parable of the prodigal son in Luke 15 wished to convey to his son (Luke 15:11-32). The father told his servants to slay "the fatted calf" and prepare a feast that would normally only be prepared for a king. In so doing the father was conveying to his son, a message something like, "My love and covenant toward you is not dependent upon your behavior or misconduct. Even though you have betrayed me and wasted your entire inheritance, I still wish to receive you with the honor normally only conveyed to a king," (Luke 15:23-24). Jesus in this parable is again conveying to us the value of covenant love unilaterally extended by this father to his son totally independent of the son's actions.

Now, it was also common custom that a part of the king's purpose in traveling throughout his land was to secure the loyalty of his subjects and rid the land of his enemies. In so doing, the king would usually travel with a large entourage of diplomatic emissaries, his harem, and his army. Part of his goal was to determine who were loyal subjects and who were rebels. How would he determine the difference? The primary indicator was the blood of a special animal poured out to welcome him at the threshold of the dwelling.

If the king saw the blood poured out at the threshold of your house, he knew that you were expressing loyalty to him and welcoming him to cross your threshold and be received in your home as a guest. If he saw no blood poured out, he knew that you were his enemy. Where blood was present on the threshold, the king would then enter (covenant cross) into that house and declare the terms of his kingdom there. Since he could not personally go to every house in every village, the king would send one of his diplomatic emissaries into the houses to which he himself could not go. However, into the homes where there was no blood poured out, the king would send his army to kill his disloyal enemies.

On occasion, the blood that was poured out on the threshold by loyal subjects was not clearly evident to the king. In such case, the king might mistake that dwelling for one occupied by disloyal enemies and send the army in to kill the inhabitants. Consequently, a custom grew up whereby when news came that a king may visit a village, the loyal villagers made sure that there was no mistaken identity. They not only poured out the blood offering on their thresholds, but they also took desert bushes, such as hyssop, dipped them in the blood and painted the blood all around the outside of the door. In so doing, it became very evident from afar off that the inhabitants of that house were loyal subjects.

This understanding of the historic eastern threshold covenant greeting custom and it application to the visit of a king is critical in understanding the events surrounding the Hebrew Passover recorded in Exodus chapter 12. I believe that many Hebrew and Christian teachers have taught this event in the opposite manner from the way in which it actually happened.

As Dr. H. Clay Trumbull so masterfully explains in his book,[5] in order to understand the events of the Passover, it is critical to understand two different Hebrew words used in the Bible, both translated in English "to pass": *abar* and *pasakh*. *Abar*

---

[5] Trumbull, H. Clay, *ibid.* pp. 209-212, 266

is used to mean "to pass by" or "to pass through," while *pasakh* means "to pass over a threshold into covenant." After the exodus of Israel from Egypt, the word *pasakh* is also used in the Bible to signify the memorial feast of Passover. Other than denoting this feast, the word *pasakh* is only used to speak of crossing over a threshold and into covenant. The word *abar*, for example is used in the passage in Exodus 34:6 in which God hid Moses in the cleft of the rock and then passed by (*abar*) in front of him. "*And the Lord passed (abar) before him and proclaimed...*" (Exodus 34:6).

The entire chapter of Exodus 12 contains the instructions that the Lord gave to the nation of Israel regarding the way in which they were to greet Him as He came to deliver His people from the slavery of Egypt. You will see that these instructions given to Israel would have been very familiar to them as eastern, covenant people. They contained the familiar greeting custom practiced upon receiving news of the potential visit of any earthly king. However, when we read these instructions, they are very strange to us, as most of us have never greeted an honored guest in this way, nor have we ever received a king in our home at all. Let's now look at a part of these instructions given in the passage in Exodus 12.

"*And thus you shall eat it: with a belt on your waist, your sandals on your feet, and your staff in your hand. So you shall eat it in haste. It is the Lord's Passover* **(Pasakh)**. *For I will pass through* **(abar)** *the land of Egypt on that night and will strike all the firstborn in the land of Egypt, both man and beast; and against all the gods of Egypt I will execute judgment; I am the Lord. Now the blood shall be a sign for you on the houses where you are. And when I see the blood, I will pass over* **(pasakh)**; *and the plague shall not be on you to destroy you when I strike the land of Egypt*" (Exodus 12:11-13).

In looking at the Hebrew words used in this passage, it dawned on me that the way I had looked at this event all of my life was exactly the opposite of the way it actually happened. I had always been taught that the Passover event had to do with the blood of the lamb being placed on the door of the house to ward God off and make sure that He didn't come into the house. The concept was more of God being a dangerous killer, Whom you want to ensure will not come into your house.

It turns out that the message that God wanted to convey to His people is just the opposite. He is coming as a king to declare to His loyal subjects (the Israelites) the terms of His Kingdom, to deliver them from slavery to the false king (Pharaoh), and to bring judgment upon His disloyal enemies (the Egyptians). So the blood of the lamb is placed upon the door of the house to invite God, the King, to covenant-cross that door and come into the house, not to avoid or "skip over" the house.

There is quite a difference in concept and relationship between placing a symbol on the outside of your home inviting an honored guest to enter and be warmly received, and that of a symbol placed to ward off an evil intruder. The obvious question then is, which picture of God more describes the relationship you have embraced with Him? Do you perceive God as someone to invite in to your home, or someone to ward off and keep out of your home? Let's have a look at one more passage in Exodus repeating these instructions and containing some more pertinent detail.

*"And you shall take a bunch of hyssop, dip it in the blood that is in the basin, and strike the lintel and the two doorposts with the blood that is in the basin. And none of you shall go out of the door of his house until morning. For the Lord will pass through **(abar)** to strike the Egyptians; and when He sees the blood on the lintel and on the two doorposts, the Lord will pass over **(pasakh)** the door and not allow the destroyer to come into your houses to strike you"* (Exodus 12:22-23).

So God told Israel that when He saw the blood on the lintel and doorposts of their homes, He would covenant-cross (*pasakh*) that door. In other words, He would come into that house and not allow the army (destroyer) to come in to harm them. He would rather instead send the destroyer (army) into the houses of the disloyal enemies who did not place the blood of the lamb on the lintel and doorposts of their houses to welcome the invading King.

Again, this concept would have been very familiar to all of Israel as the common custom of the time for greeting a conquering king. By giving instructions according to natural customs, God was able to very easily convey to the Israelites His intentions to come to them as a deliverer and a conquering King, to free them from their oppressive captors and to bring judgment upon the enemies of the King. Whereas these would have been very familiar instructions to Israel at that time, they are very foreign and strange to us reading them now. This is why most of us have misunderstood the Passover and thought that the blood on the doorpost was to keep God out of the house, rather than to invite Him into the house.

Understanding the New Covenant

Once we understand the eastern concept of threshold covenant and the Israelite Passover, we are now prepared to understand the New Covenant made by the blood of Jesus the Messiah. You see, Jesus did not come to bring us the Word of God, to be a prophet, or to be an example to us of how to live. Jesus came to give up his life and pour out His blood at the threshold of His Father's eternal dwelling. In the New Covenant, God Almighty reverses the roles from the Hebrew Passover. He now says, "I wish to treat you as a king, and to invite you to step across the threshold where the most precious blood in the universe is poured out. This is not the blood of a goat, a bullock, or even 'the fatted calf.' The blood I have poured out is not representative blood, but rather is My own blood poured out through Jesus Christ."

In the Passover, God asked the Hebrew people to pour out the representative blood of a lamb and invite Him as the King to covenant-cross their thresholds. In the New Covenant, God has poured out the blood of THE LAMB at the threshold of His eternal dwelling, and then like the prodigal son's father, He desires to treat us as a king, and has invited us to step across the blood on the threshold of His dwelling. When we do so, we enter into blood covenant with Him, thus obtaining all the benefits and obligations of a threshold covenant.

This New Covenant is spoken of in Jeremiah 31:31-34:

*Behold the days are coming says the Lord, **when I will make a new covenant** with the house of Israel and with the house of Judah—not according to the covenant that I made with their fathers in the day that I took then by the hand to lead them out of the land of Egypt, My covenant which they broke, though I was a husband to them, says the Lord. But this is the covenant that I will make with the house of Israel after those days, says the Lord: I will put My law in their minds and write it on their hearts; and I will be their God, and they shall be My people. No more shall every man teach his neighbor, and every man his brother saying, 'Know the Lord,' for they shall all know Me, from the least of them to the greatest of them, says the Lord. For I will forgive their iniquity, and their sin I will remember no more"* (Jeremiah 31:31-34).

So, now understanding a little more about the threshold covenant, we can understand that God has offered us the opportunity to personally step across the threshold of His eternal dwelling by the blood of Messiah. He has also offered us the opportunity to step across this threshold as a married couple and subject our marriage and family to the protection, provision, and promises that He has made available by covenant.

In conclusion, we must understand that the message of this chapter is two-fold. Firstly, you have an opportunity to recommit your marriage to the value of covenant, putting back in place in your marriage the strength and security depicted by the eastern threshold covenant. Secondly, you have an opportunity together as a married couple to step across the threshold of God's eternal dwelling, across the shed blood of His Son, Jesus the Messiah, and into the strength and security of His New Covenant with you.

If you would like to, I invite you to pray together as a couple the following prayer to dedicate your personal lives and marriage together to God in covenant.

"Father God, thank you for pouring out the blood of Jesus Christ for us at the threshold of Your eternal dwelling. Thank you for your New Covenant and your willingness to forgive all of our iniquity and to remember ours sins no more as we enter into that covenant."

"So as individuals and as a married couple, right now by faith we take that step across the threshold of your eternal dwelling and enter into Your New Covenant. Forgive us for all of our past mistakes, iniquities and sins. We receive Your forgiveness by the blood of Jesus Christ. In stepping across Your threshold, we receive Your total authority and rulership in our lives and marriage, and make ourselves Your servants. All we have, and all we are, we give to you today. We commit our lives and our marriage to Your purposes, and we give You permission to do anything You desire with and in our lives. Thank you for receiving us into Your New Covenant. Amen."

Reflection

1. A blood covenant of hospitality was established between host and guest upon the crossing of the threshold of the dwelling by the guest.

2. Blood was always poured out by the host at the threshold of the dwelling to welcome the guest.

3. The guest was obligated to step over the blood on the threshold and not to step in it, which would have been a great insult to the host. In stepping across he was acknowledging submission to the authority and hospitality of the host.

4. The host was obligated to support and protect the guest even to the extent of his own life and the life of his family.

5. In marriage, the husband becomes like the host and the bride like the guest in the eastern threshold covenant understanding.

6. In the Hebrew Passover, God as a conquering King comes to the Israelite people to declare the terms of the kingdom and to lead the people out of bondage and slavery to the Egyptians.

7. In so doing God requires the Israelites to prepare to enter into the threshold blood covenant with God their King, just as they would for the coming of any earthly king.

8. God then steps across the sacrificial blood on the threshold of each Israelite home and enters into threshold covenant with the inhabitants of that home. He then sends the army (death angel) into the homes of His enemies where there is no blood poured out at the threshold to welcome Him.

9. In the New Covenant, God has reversed the roles and has poured out His own blood through Jesus Christ at the threshold of His eternal dwelling. He now invites us to step across and partake of all of the promises, protection, and provision, that comes as His blood covenant partners from our stepping across His threshold and abiding under His authority in His household.

10. Have you personally and as a couple stepped across the threshold of God's eternal dwelling and submitted your lives and marriage by blood covenant to His authority, rulership, promises, protection and provision?

Resources

☐ *An Ancient Paths Seminar:* Covenant Marriage (Covenant Marriage Retreat). See Appendix for details and www.familyfoundations.com for schedule of upcoming events.

🎧 The Secrets of the Blood Covenant

chapter 5
Our Marriage
Journey

I would now like to share with you a little bit of our own personal journey in marriage. When Jan and I married, we truly were free in certain areas, but unfortunately we were fleas in other areas. We both had personally entered into New Covenant relationship with God and had dedicated the rest of our lives to serving Him. Neither of us were looking for a marriage partner when we met, but were rather quite focused on the mission to which we had been called at the time. Thus in the summer of 1975, we found ourselves together on a Youth With a Mission team carrying Russian and Polish Bibles from Germany into Poland. Poland and Russia were still in communist hands at that time, and it was not possible to openly send or take Bibles to believers in those countries.

We both began to realize while on the mission team that God had stirred a romantic interest in us toward each other, but since at that time we needed to be single minded and focused on our mission, we agreed not to pursue the relationship until we both returned to the United States. In addition, I wanted to meet and secure the blessing of Jan's parents before I allowed the relationship to move beyond a friendship.

When we returned to the U.S in the autumn of that year, I met Jan's parents, and her father opened the door for us to begin a romantic relationship toward the goal of marriage. We both had about a year and a half of university to finish and fortunately Jan's parents lived right in between the two universities we were attending. So, about every three weeks we were able to meet at Jan's parents' home for the weekend and get to know each other more.

Low Fuel

In the course of talking with each other, I was very surprised to find out that God had led Jan to pray for me in a very specific way six months before we had even met. Although she didn't know at the time that it was me she was praying for, God had led her in a very supernatural way to participate in saving my life. Let me share with you how that had happened.

In early 1975, I had just graduated from college and had a nine-month period of time before I would start a two-year graduate MBA program in Chicago. For the first few months of the year, I was employed as a copilot in a Learjet flying the US mail out of Grand Rapids, Michigan five nights a week. We would leave Grand Rapids around midnight and fly to Chicago, Bloomington, Illinois and on to St. Louis. Then we would fly back through Peoria, Illinois, Chicago again and then back across Lake Michigan to Grand Rapids. One night, on the last leg of the trip from Chicago back to Grand Rapids, the Chicago Air Traffic Control Center advised us that the weather in much of Michigan was deteriorating very rapidly with fog and low visibility. He suggested that we might want to return to Chicago.

The captain and I looked at each other, and he asked me, "Do you want to go back to Chicago?"

"No," I answered. "If we do, we'll probably get stuck in the pilots' lounge all day. I'm tired. I want to go home and go to bed. I bet we can beat the fog into Grand Rapids."

He concurred with me. We told the Air Traffic Control that we would continue to Grand Rapids.

I don't know why, but I have noticed that frequently they locate airports right in the crook of a river. This is the case in Grand Rapids, Michigan. So where does the fog form first? Right over the river of course, which is right on the approach end of the precision instrument approach runway. As a result, we had discovered that when the visibility was low, many times we could get into the airport on the non-precision instrument approach from the non-river end of the runway more easily even though the visibility and altitude minimums were higher than they were from the other direction.

This particular night, we shot the first instrument approach with no success. When we arrived at the minimum altitude we saw no runway, no lights, no ground; nothing but fog. So we ascended and tried the precision approach from the other direction. On descent on the second approach two little red lights illuminated on our panel, "LOW FUEL." Unfortunately the second approach yielded the same results as the first. Now we both knew that we had made a mistake. We asked the controllers what was the closest airport that was still above visibility minimums. They responded that Lansing, Michigan was still open.

So, we headed for Lansing as fast as we could go. Unfortunately, with the type of jet engines that powered this Learjet, we were burning at low altitude about 4 times as much fuel as we burned at cruise altitude. When we arrived at Lansing, we again shot an instrument approach from each of two directions to the minimum altitude, but the fog was already too thick to allow us to see the runway lights. Now we were really low on fuel. We asked the controller what other airport near us was open. He told us Detroit, but added that the visibility was going down fast there, too.

I was now beginning to really fear for my life. As we flew over to Detroit, I was having visions of heaven and talking with the saints of old. I could just see myself conversing with Abraham, Moses, and Peter.

"And how did you die, Peter?" I queried.

"Well," he said, "I was crucified upside-down for the name of Christ. And how did you die, Craig?"

"I was stupid and ran out of fuel in an airplane," I reluctantly had to admit. I really did not want to have that testimony for all of eternity.

When we finally arrived in Detroit, we were the second to the last airplane to make it into the Detroit airport before the fog reduced the visibility below minimums at that airport also. We landed with literally only minutes of fuel left.

One Old, One Young - Blue Flight Suits

Later in July of that year, as I mentioned earlier, I met Jan on the team in Europe. Through the autumn of that year we continued to meet at Jan's parents home every third weekend or so. During this time of getting to know each other, I was relating to Jan the various "heroic" events of my life. One evening at her parents' home I was sharing with her how I had almost run out of fuel and crashed in a Learjet in Michigan earlier that year. As the story unfolded a surprised look came upon Jan's face and as I finished, she remarked, "I have to ask you two questions."

"What are those?" I replied.

"Was the other pilot quite a bit older than you?"

"Yes." I replied.

"Were you both wearing light blue, one-piece flight suits?"

"Yes," I replied. "But why would you ask that?"

"We prayed for you!" she announced.

"What do you mean, 'you prayed for me?' This happened in January. I didn't even meet you until July. How could you have prayed for me, when you didn't even know me yet?"

Then Jan began to explain. At that time in January 1975, Jan had been part of a YWAM School of Evangelism in Germany. Every morning the students met in small groups for prayer. During the course of their school, a dynamic intercessor and Bible teacher, Joy Dawson, had taught the students a particular prayer model. Usually when people pray, they simply pray for their "shopping list" of all the things that they would like God to help them with. They just pray for the things that are important to them.

In this YWAM school Joy Dawson had taught the students to ask the Lord what was on His heart that day that He would like them to pray. (For more understanding of this method of prayer you may want to listen to the CD teaching entitled, *Why Pray?*[1].) It was their understanding that they were to partner with God in prayer to release His authority on earth to accomplish His purposes.

Consequently, every morning in their small groups the students would first ask the Lord what He wanted for them to pray. They would then share the topics that came to their minds with each other and make a list of these topics. They then proceeded to take each topic one by one and ask the Lord what they were to pray. Frequently the Holy Spirit would bring to their minds things to pray of which they had no natural cognitive knowledge. Sometimes they would then receive confirmation from natural sources regarding the things that they had prayed, but most

---

[1] Craig Hill, *Why Pray? Littleton, CO, Family Foundations International,* 2003, CD can be purchased at www.familyfoundations.com

times they did not. Each day they were simply faithful to pray what God brought to their minds as a group.

Jan shared with me that one day back in January as they were initially asking the Lord what they were to pray for that day, one of the topics that came up was that they were to pray for an airplane. As they prayed through the list of topics they had for the morning, as was their custom, when they came to the topic "airplane," they naturally asked the Lord, "What are we supposed to pray about an airplane?"

Then one by one each member of the group shared and prayed what came to their minds regarding this topic.

One person said, "I sense that the airplane we are to pray for is very small, but very fast like United" (a U.S. airline company).

Another one contributed, "I sense that there are only two pilots on board. One is old and one is young."

Someone else said, "I see that the two pilots are both wearing light blue one-piece flight suits and they are carrying the U.S. mail."

Jan shared, "I am seeing a map picture of the western part of the Great Lakes area of the United States. The map appears very dark and is growing foggier. I believe the plane is running out of gas, and we need to pray for them to find a place to land."

The group then proceeded to pray for this airplane and for a safe place for it to land. They prayed until they felt like the Holy Spirit had exhausted everything they were to pray for this topic and the job was complete. They then went on to the next topic, which was China, or something that seemed more important in the Kingdom of God.

Jan further related to me that she would not have remembered this specific instance of prayer, as they prayed for things for which they had no natural knowledge every day, so this day was not particularly notable. However, after the prayer time that day, another one of the students who was a member of that small group approached Jan and told her, "Jan, I sense that airplane we prayed for has something to do with you."

Jan thought for a moment and then replied, "I don't really know anyone who is involved with airplanes. I am from small town Iowa. There was a farmer I knew who had a small airplane, that I heard he sometimes flew in and out of his cornfield. But I don't really think it has anything to do with him. I really can't think of anyone else right now."

The other girl in the group said, "Well, I don't know. I just sensed that I was supposed to tell you that."

Jan told me that she wasn't sure what to do with that information, but she trusted the spiritual insights that this girl often got from the Lord. Consequently, she just shelved it in the back of her mind.

As I was sharing my experience, the Holy Spirit brought that incidence of prayer, and what the other girl in the group had said back to Jan's remembrance and that is why she announced to me, "We prayed for you!" We couldn't confirm the exact date, but we knew the prayer and the incident had both taken place in January. We also realized that because of the time zone difference between Germany and Michigan, the time Jan and her group were praying was about the same time that we were having the problem. As Jan shared this incident, I was amazed that God had used the young woman who would be my future wife to pray for me and participate in saving my life six months before we even met.

Married

After we both completed our university studies, in April of 1977, Jan and I were married. On our wedding day, we both had a very good understanding of unilateral, unconditional covenant in marriage. Neither of us believed in a contract type of marriage. As a matter of fact we had somewhat of a humorous incident occur at our wedding regarding this. The preacher we had invited to marry us did not know our family members well. However, in his message at our wedding he was talking about marriage being a life-long covenant and his certainty that Jan and I had that understanding. He went on to say that many people getting married are so uncertain of the future of their marriage that they visit a lawyer to conclude a prenuptial agreement, just in case it "doesn't work out."

He went on to say, "I'm certain that these kids haven't even been near a lawyer." What the preacher did not realize, was that Jan's sister, who was her maid of honor, was a lawyer. So all of her family who knew that began to chuckle, since we were at that very moment standing right next to a lawyer.

Since Jan and I both embraced marriage as a covenant, divorce was not something either of us ever considered. Since we both loved the Lord, we knew God had led us together to be married, and we planned to spend our lives ministering to others, I think we both assumed that our marriage relationship would be easy. However, this turned out not to be the case. From the beginning, we began to offend and wound each other.

> I think we both assumed that our marriage relationship would be easy. However, this turned out not to be the case.

It always seemed to me that Jan would become offended over nothing and then close up, refuse to talk to me and act as if I were the "bad guy."

I thought, "Why do you treat me as if I am the bad guy when out of the blue, for no apparent reason, you manifest some totally unwarranted emotional response, then close up and reject me. You're obviously the one with the problem, not me."

From Jan's standpoint, she felt that that I made comments that would judge, shame and condemn her. When she attempted to point this out to me, I would justify myself and further condemn her. So she would close up and withdraw to protect herself. She could not understand how I could be so prideful, cutting, judgmental, and insensitive towards her and then refuse to apologize or even acknowledge that I had done anything wrong.

For seven years, neither of us honestly had any idea how to stop emotionally wounding each other. I remember that there were more than four years when we literally couldn't pray together without me hurting Jan and her closing up. So we didn't pray. We also didn't talk on a very deep level for the same reason. We both knew we were called to minister to others, but we couldn't do that since we couldn't even stop wounding each other or pray together. Our plans to move to Russia or Eastern Europe completely died. We had nothing to export to others except frustration, emotional pain, anger, and depression.

> Neither of us understood that we were just pawns being used by a common enemy in a battle much greater than ourselves.

I remember crying out to God for help, but it seemed like nothing happened. I knew that I must be part of the problem and I was very willing to change. The only problem was that I just could not see in what area I needed to change. I knew that I could not move forward in ministry without Jan, but at that time we could not move forward together. I knew that I had to learn how to stop wounding my wife and bless her before I could legitimately minister to anyone else.

Because we had no understanding of the spiritual warfare involved in marriage, we each thought that the other was the enemy and needed to change. We each thought, "How can you say you love me and then treat me like this?" Neither of us understood that we were just pawns being used by a common enemy in a battle much greater than ourselves.

Jan and I saw each other as the only players involved in our conflict. We had no understanding that the kingdom of darkness had set up a self-destructive scheme in our lives that was very effective in damaging our marriage relationship. This scheme was predicated upon keeping us blind to a certain level of communication. We would then communicate on that level a very wounding message to each other, but remain totally blind to the fact that we had done so.

Think for a moment from the standpoint of the kingdom of darkness, whose purpose it is to destroy your marriage and family relationships. What if the devil through your own blindness can get you to communicate to your spouse that he is totally worthless in your sight and that you don't love or respect him? Furthermore, what if this scheme works through your own blindness in such a way that you are totally unaware that you have communicated this message? That is exactly what happens in most marriages. What a great strategy!

This was the strategy that effectively worked in our marriage for the first seven years. When Jan would confront me with the relational message I was sending her, I would deny it because I was really unaware of it. I then felt as if she were falsely accusing me, so I would defend and justify. She would then give up and withdraw in hopelessness that I would ever take responsibility for hurting her and apologize. I, of course, was still not able to do so because I couldn't see that I had done anything wrong.

As a result of the outworking of this strategy, for the first several years of our marriage, Jan frequently felt devalued and unloved, and I frequently felt falsely accused and unacceptable in her sight. Finally after suffering in our relationship for seven years, we had a major breakthrough when we discovered the principles outlined in the next chapter. I have chronicled a much more detailed account of the understanding I finally received, in my book *Deceived, Who Me?*[2]

Reflection

1. God knew we would be married from the foundation of time and planned exciting ways to introduce us to each other.

2. Even though we both loved God, loved each other, had a purpose and destiny greater than ourselves to fulfill, we still struggled in our marriage and wounded each other deeply for the first 7 years.

3. We realized that God's order requires that marriage must be a priority even above ministry or service to God.

4. It violates integrity and God's order for one called to ministry to attempt to move forward in ministry independent of resolving marital conflict and establishing intimacy and true heart to heart communication with a spouse.

5. Breakthrough came for us through perseverance and diligence in seeking God and working on our marriage relationship.

Resources

Bondage Broken

Deceived, Who Me?

Why Pray?

---

[2] Hill, Craig, *Deceived, Who Me?*, Littleton, Family Foundations International, 1986

c h a p t e r 6
Miscommunication:
Schemes
of the Devil

"*F*inally, *be strong in the Lord, and in the strength of His might. Put on the full armor of God, that you may be able to stand firm against **the schemes of the devil**. For our struggle is not against flesh and blood, but against the rulers, against the powers, against the world forces of this darkness, against the spiritual forces of wickedness in heavenly places*" (Ephesians 6:10-12).

As I mentioned above, the devil and the kingdom of darkness have specific schemes through which they work. A "scheme of the devil" is a premeditated, well-thought-out plan devised to deceive and destroy you. When we look at a marriage, we see that the purpose of God is to take the two and make them one. The devil is always seeking to do the opposite of what God is doing. So his purpose is to take the unity of a marriage and divide the couple into two.

The purpose of the devil in perpetrating his schemes against a couple is to create division. Di is a Latin prefix meaning "two." So di—vision means two visions, or to see two different things. The purpose of the devil is to get a husband and wife to have two different visions, or to see things in two totally different ways. If they each have a separate vision, then that couple can never come together and pursue one vision. They always find themselves in division, thus fulfilling the purpose of the enemy. Let's now look at a specific scheme that works very effectively in many marriages to cause a husband and wife to not only be divided but to actually verbally and emotionally shoot at each other as enemies.

> Di–vision means two visions, or to see two different things

Shot By the Arms Dealer

I remember seeing a movie some years ago that I thought illustrated this point about as well as any. It was a movie about the American Revolution in 1776, and the first shot of the war, which they termed as "the shot heard around the world." I actually don't now remember the name of the movie, and I have no idea as to whether the contents were historically accurate or not. However, the scene depicted in the movie, as I remember it, was very descriptive of what I believe takes place in many marriages.

The movie depicted the British soldiers marching up the road to Concord and Lexington. They were confronted by a column of American colonist militia. The two armies were facing each other with guns at the ready. The commander from each side came out to meet and talk with each other.

Unbeknownst to anyone, there was an arms dealer hiding behind a stone wall in the bushes. He really had no interest in the politics or issues of either side. He simply wanted to initiate a war so that he could sell arms to both sides.

As the two generals were discussing together, the arms dealer from behind the wall took aim and shot the second in command British officer dead. Immediately the talks between the two commanders ceased and the British commander ordered his soldiers to return a volley of fire back against the American colonists. The Americans, of course then returned a volley back against the British, and the war was on.

This movie depicted "the shot heard around the world," then, as a shot that was not fired by either side, but rather by a third party in whose interest it was to start a war. I think that this episode very accurately depicts what commonly happens in the lives of many married couples. I have asked many couples in conflict if either of them intentionally started the conflict. Both parties have assured me that it was the other one who started it and refuses to apologize or take responsibility for it. After understanding this Ephesians 6:10-12 passage, I now realize that from their perception, both husband and wife are correct. Neither of them intentionally started the conflict. It really was started by a disinterested third party (the devil), who had a vested interest in initiating a conflict.

Think for a moment about the perspectives of the two opposing commanders in the American Revolution scenario described above. If you were to ask the American commander, "Did you fire the first shot," he would conclusively answer, "No, we were suddenly fired upon by the British for no apparent reason." He would have said this because he knew that none of his men had fired the shot, and he had no knowledge of the shot fired by the hidden arms dealer.

If you were to ask the British commander, "Did you fire the first shot, he would vehemently answer, "No, our officer was shot and killed by the Americans with no prior provocation whatsoever." Again, the British commander was not at all aware of the presence and actions of the arms dealer. In such a situation, neither side will take responsibility for firing upon the other without provocation. Both sides will maintain that the other side fired first, and each was merely returning fire in self-defense.

This is exactly what was happening in our marriage for the first seven years. The enemy would take a shot at one of us through the other without either realizing it. Neither of us then was able to recognize our part in the conflict and thus take responsibility to solve it. Both Jan and I would continue to maintain, "I have done nothing wrong and I am waiting for my spouse to take responsibility and apologize for firing upon me without provocation." As a result, we each waited seven years for the other to repent, and resolved very few conflicts during that time.

Topical vs. Relational

So if we have no recognition of the scheme of the devil operating, then each of us will believe the lies that "This other person really is my problem, and my battle really is against my spouse." Secondly we believe, "Since I am not at fault, I have no responsibility in this and don't need to repent or apologize."

After seven years of this scheme operating in our marriage, I finally began to get an understanding of how the enemy was using me to shoot Jan, and not realize it. I discovered that this scheme of the devil was working through my blindness to a particular level of communication.

People who study communication talk about seven levels of communication. However, I have found that in order to understand this particular scheme, it is really only necessary to understand two levels of communication:

1) Topical Communication; and

2) Relational Communication

I have come to define Topical Communication as: Messages we send to one another regarding various topics or external issues of life. For example, a couple may discuss where to live, what house to buy or rent, what jobs to hold, where to take a vacation, how to manage their money, how to discipline children, division of labor within the household, or how to conduct their sexual relationship. Discussion about all of these issues is topical in nature.

Underlying all Topical Communication is Relational Communication. I would define this as: **Underlying messages we send to one another in the realm of identity regarding value.** At any moment in time, I can send my wife or any other person an underlying message, "You are very valuable. You are worth spending time with. Your opinions count. Your feelings matter to me." Or I can send someone the message, "You are totally worthless. You are not worth spend-

> I have found that the primary scheme of the devil is to use unseen relational communication between husband and wife to wound and damage relationship, but then to keep both parties completely blind to its existence.

ing time with. Your opinions don't count, and your feelings don't matter to me." These are relational communication messages and usually produce very potent emotional responses in others.

I have found that the primary scheme of the devil is to use unseen relational communication between husband and wife to wound and damage relationship, but then to keep both parties completely blind to its existence.

I have heard the statistic that only 7% of a communicated message is contained in the words spoken. Another 38% is in the voice intonation, and 55% is in the body language. If this is true, then 93% (38% voice intonation + 55% body language) of a communicated message is non-verbal. Most wives know this, but don't know how to explain it. Most husbands don't know this. Husbands usually focus on the words used. "All I said was …" The wife will then state, "It's not what he said that hurt. It was <u>how he said it</u>." What was the "how?" This was the underlying relational message.

A very common scenario in marriage is that a husband will go out of his way to do something extra, special, or kind for his wife because he wants to let her know how much he loves and cares about her. However, in the process of doing so, he will inadvertently and unknowingly be used by the "arms dealer" to shoot his wife and send her a relational message that she is worthless. She, then being wounded from the relational message, will feel very unloved and uncared for, but will not have language to explain to him what just happened. In her pain, she will exclaim, "You don't love me. You don't care about me!"

This language is totally confusing to her husband since he has just gone out of his way to try to bless her and show her that he does love and care about her. In fact this language carries a relational message from his wife to him that despite his efforts to love her and please her, he is still unacceptable in her sight, and a miserable failure as a husband and a man.

His conclusion then, is that nothing he ever does will please her, so what's the use in even trying. Her conclusion is that he really doesn't love or care about her because nobody could do what he just did and not even apologize if he loved or cared about his wife. **It doesn't dawn on either of them that perhaps the other person is actually blind rather than malicious**, and the "arms dealer" has won by starting a war.

Love and Respect

So, the primary scheme of the devil is to use us to send a spouse a relational message, "You're worthless," without realizing that we have done so. Because husbands and wives tend to perceive value in totally different ways, the way the message is conveyed from one to the other is a little different in each case.

We are instructed in Ephesians 5:33 that a husband is **to love his wife**, and that a wife is **to respect her husband**. *"Nevertheless, let each one of you in particular so love his own wife as himself, and let the wife see that she respects her husband"* (Ephesians 5:33). I believe that Apostle Paul expressed the instruction this way to reflect the difference in perception of value between a husband and wife. Wives tend to feel value through love, while husbands tend to feel value through respect.

As I have thought about the couples we have ministered to, I was able to come up with some very simple definitions for love and respect. In order to convey love to a wife, a husband must convey that she is **high priority** to him and that her opinions and feelings matter. In order to convey respect to a husband, a wife must convey to him that he is **acceptable, adequate, and a success** in her sight. A husband conveys lack of love when he makes his wife low priority in his schedule or invalidates her feelings through focus on the topical communication with no regard for her heart. A wife conveys lack of respect when she criticizes her husband or refuses to acknowledge his efforts to try to please her.

In his book *The Marriage Builder,*[1] Dr. Lawrence Crabb gives further insight as to why husbands crave respect and wives crave love. He states that there are two basic longings inside every person in the realm of the identity. These are: 1) **Security** and 2) **Significance**. Dr. Crabb defines these as follows: "Security: a convinced awareness of being unconditionally and totally loved without needing to change in order to win love, loved by a love that is freely given, that cannot be earned and therefore cannot be lost." "Significance: a realization that I am engaged in a responsibility or job that is truly important, whose results will not evaporate with time, but will last through eternity, that

---

1 Lawrence J. Crabb, Jr., The Marriage Builder, Grand Rapids, MI: Zondervan, 1982 pp. 80 - 81

fundamentally involves having a meaningful impact on another person, a job for which I am completely adequate."

Dr. Crabb also discusses the fact that although security and significance are important for both marriage partners, the deeper need of the wife is usually in the realm of security and the deeper need of the husband in the realm of significance. So the conveyance of love from a husband tends to meet the security need of a wife and make her feel valuable, while the conveyance of respect from a wife tends to meet the significance need of a husband and make him feel valuable.

A husband primarily conveys love to his wife through sending her a message on the relational level that she as a person is valuable to him, and that she is high priority to him above all other persons and activities. She must know that her opinions, her feelings, and her words are important to him.

A wife, on the other hand, primarily conveys respect to her husband through sending him a message on the relational level acknowledging his efforts to please her, that he is adequate as a husband, and is accepted in her sight. He must know that he is significant and respected in her eyes.

Consequently, the most frequent complaint that I have heard a wife express regarding her husband is that he doesn't listen and isn't involved in her life. A husband often invalidates identity by quickly offering logical solutions instead of offering empathy. She thinks, "**He doesn't really love me.** He doesn't ever listen to me, think about me or include me in his life. He's very selfish. I am number 9,999 on his priority list. He pursues his career, ministry, friends, hobbies, sports, TV and everything else before me. I don't mean anything to him. If I died tomorrow, his life would go on unchanged, except that he would need to hire a housekeeper, babysitter, launderer, and cook. No matter what I do, he doesn't care about me, and I just can't get him to listen include me, or pay any attention to me."

The most frequent complaint I have heard from a husband regarding his wife is that she is always trying to change him. A wife often invalidates identity through criticism instead of offering acceptance. He thinks, **"She doesn't really honor or respect me.** I am obviously not what she wants or desires as a husband. She frequently makes me feel foolish, inadequate, unappreciated and displeasing. I can't do anything pleasing in her sight. When I go out of my way to do something extra or special for her, she still complains; is displeased with something, and I end up being a failure again in her sight. Even if I spent all my time, energy and money trying to please her, she still wouldn't be happy. In her sight I am just an inadequate husband, father and man."

The State Fair

One of the most poignant examples of this scheme of the devil at work in a marriage was shared with us recently by some good friends of ours. Tom and Sue, when this event occurred, had been married over 30 years and had four children. Having worked through many issues in their marriage, Tom and Sue felt that they were communicating quite well in their relationship with each other. However, the scheme of using each other to convey lack of love and lack of respect on a relational level was still occasionally at work.

Sue and several of her close friends had arranged to go out of town together a couple hours away for a weekend retreat. She had asked Tom if he would watch their four children for the weekend while she was away. While the two older children were teenagers, the two younger ones still needed fairly close supervision by a parent. Tom was happy to spend the time with his children and let Sue have the retreat time with her friends.

The weekend progressed well for both Tom and Sue. On Saturday evening, Tom's older son said to his dad, "What are we going to do tomorrow afternoon, Dad?"

Tom had a pretty good idea of what he was planning to do. His hometown NFL team was playing football the next afternoon, and Tom had been looking forward to watching the game for some time. However, the state fair had just begun that weekend, and Tom's older son announced, "Hey Dad, we could go to the state fair tomorrow afternoon!"

Every year Tom's family always went together as a family to the state fair, as it was a large and exciting event. The older kids loved riding the rides, and the younger girls loved the games and winning the little prizes. One of the other kids heard the comment and chimed in, "Yeah, Dad, let's go to the fair tomorrow!"

Well, there went the football game. However, Tom loved his children and delighted in pleasing them, so he decided to deny himself and take the kids to the state fair. So Sunday afternoon, Tom and his children headed off to the fair. When they arrived, the older two immediately bolted for the bigger rides. The younger two headed with their dad to the game booths.

While Tom was entertaining his youngest two daughters with the games, his cell phone rang. It was Sue on the other end, just checking in to see how everything was going.

"What's that noise I hear in the background?" Sue remarked. "Sounds like you're out at a park or somewhere."

"Oh, yeah, the kids talked me into taking them to the state fair," replied Tom.

"The state fair!" cried Sue in shock and disbelief. "Why did you take the kids to the fair?"

"Well, because they asked," replied Tom. He could tell by the tone in Sue's voice that he was now in trouble. However, he didn't have a clue why.

"But we always go to the state fair together as a family. Why didn't you call me and tell me you were going to the fair this afternoon?" asked Sue.

"Because you were away with your friends on a retreat and I didn't want to bother you," replied Tom.

"But I was only two hours away, and if I knew that you were going to the fair, I might have chosen to come home early and go with you. Every year we go to the fair as a family," declared Sue.

"Yeah, but this isn't the only time we can go to the fair. We could go again next weekend together," quickly offered Tom.

"No, it won't be the same, because now the kids have already gone once this year. Why couldn't you have just picked up the phone and let me know you were thinking of going to the fair today?" requested Sue.

"I don't know. It just didn't dawn on me to call you," replied Tom.

"Well, didn't it dawn on you that I am a part of the family, and that if the family is going to the fair, that I might like to be included?" asked Sue.

"No, it didn't dawn on me. I actually wanted to stay home and watch the football game, but I decided to deny my own desire and bless the kids today. I didn't think to call you. I had no idea that trying to bless my children would be some huge offence to you," retorted Tom.

"So the truth is, that I don't even matter. You don't care about me. You don't even remember I'm a part of the family. I'm not even included in your thinking when you plan a family event," angrily said Sue.

"Well I guess I should have just told the kids to forget it when they asked about the fair and stayed home and watched football. If I would have done that, then you'd be happy, and I wouldn't be the evil, selfish, uncaring husband that you claim I am," replied Tom.

By this time the volume and intensity of voice intonation had significantly elevated for both Tom and Sue. Both of them

were hurt and angry. Tom was completely taken off guard. Here
he was denying his own desire to watch the game for the sake of
blessing his children. He would have thought that when Sue
found out about his noble act, she might be calling to issue him
the "father of the year award," not to tell him what an unfeeling,
disappointing and unacceptable husband he was. This was totally
unintelligible to Tom. Why was it that no matter what he did, he
was always still the "bad guy" in his wife's eyes? We have found
that this type of experience is definitely not unique to Tom and
Sue.

From Sue's perspective, how could it be that Tom was so
dense, unfeeling, uncaring that he didn't even consider that she
might like to come home and join the family in an annual "family outing" to the state fair. Every year in the past they had
always gone to the fair together as a family. How could it not
dawn on Tom that going to the fair is a family event, and that
she would want to be included as a part of the family. Her
thoughts went something similar to the following: "He just
doesn't seem to notice or care about me, my feelings, or the
things that might be important to me. He honors and supports
everybody else ahead of me. He acts as if I don't exist or at least
don't matter, except in the areas in which I in some way serve
his goals. He doesn't really think of or care about me."

Unfortunately, Tom and Sue deeply wounded each other and
were not able to resolve this miscommunication for a couple of
weeks. This is a classic example of how the scheme of the devil
functions. If we ask the question, who started this conflict, and
who was at fault, we find that neither Tom, nor Sue planned to
wound the other or initiate a "war." They were both set up by
the "arms dealer" behind the wall. Tom felt that he was "fired
upon" by Sue with no prior provocation, and for no apparent
reason. Sue felt that she was fired upon by Tom, by being
excluded from the family at an annual family activity.

In reality, the kingdom of darkness took advantage of an
unavoidable situation to convince Tom and Sue that they were

each other's enemy, and to further shoot at each other. At that moment both of them were blind to the relational level of communication. Neither Tom nor Sue recognized that they were a part of an Ephesians 6:10-12 scheme of the devil. It didn't dawn on either of them that they had been set up by a common enemy (the arms dealer) and that he had gotten them to shoot at each other and to become each other's enemy. Honestly, Ephesians 6:10-12 might as well not have been written for all the good it does most couples in the heat of the moment.

Since Jan and I began to understand what was happening to us, we discovered two very specific lies through which the scheme was functioning in our marriage. These lies were the following.

1. **"When a disagreement between us begins, my problem really is my spouse."** Ephesians 6:12 states that our struggle is not against flesh and blood. But the first lie we often get drawn into believing is that the struggle really is against this other flesh and blood person.

2. **"Since I'm right about this issue, and my partner is wrong and needs to change, I have no need to apologize or ask forgiveness."** The deception here is that you may be actually right about the topical issue, but the shot fired was not on the topical level. It was on the relational level, and on that level you are wrong because you have shot and wounded someone and therefore need to repent and ask forgiveness.

Bad Husband

Let's look at the inadvertent relational messages conveyed in the above example. Without realizing it, by taking his children to the state fair without at least consulting or inviting Sue, the enemy had been able to convey a relational message through Tom to her of "You don't count. You're not a part of the family. You are very low priority to Tom and don't even enter into his thinking or planning. Tom doesn't love or care about you." Now this message would wound anyone. The problem was that Tom was not aware that this message had been sent to his wife, because he was blind to the relational level of communication.

On the other hand, when Sue called and discovered that Tom and the kids were at the fair, the enemy then used her to convey a relational message to Tom, "You are a huge disappointment to me. You are totally insensitive and discourteous. You don't care about me or love me. I don't accept you or receive you. You are not what I want or need. You are a massive failure in my sight as a husband and man." Again, Sue had no idea that the enemy had just used her to deeply wound, dishonor, and reject her husband, because she was also blind to the relational level of communication at that moment.

> Ephesians 5:33 instructs the husband to love his wife and the wife to respect her husband, because wives have a core need to be loved, and husbands have a core need to be respected

Remember that Ephesians 5:33 instructs the husband to love his wife and the wife to respect her husband, because wives have a core need to be loved, and husbands have a core need to be respected. Love primarily means to be considered high priority and for the feelings of a wife to be foremost in the mind of her husband. So, in this instance, without realizing it, the true enemy had used Tom to convey to Sue, "Not only are you not high priority in my thinking, but you don't even enter into my thinking." In this way she was made to feel not loved.

Respect primarily means to be made to feel accepted, received, not a disappointment, but a blessing. Another word for respect is honor. To further understand this let's look at the meaning of this word "honor" in another context. If you go to a restaurant and the sign at the cash register says, "We honor

MasterCard®," what does that mean? It means, "Here we accept and receive MasterCard®. We consider it valid and legitimate to perform its function here." I think that this is the primary core desire of every husband of his wife. To be respected or honored would mean that he would receive from his wife the relational message, "You are a good husband. I accept and receive you. You are not a disappointment, but rather a blessing. I consider you a valid and legitimate husband."

So without realizing it, in the above instance the enemy used Sue to disrespect and dishonor Tom by conveying to him the relational message that he was a "bad husband," unacceptable and a disappointment in her sight.

You Don't Matter

To make the relational messages that convey love and respect very simple, I would say that the message a wife wants to receive is, **"you and your feelings matter to me."** The message a husband wants to receive is, **"good husband."**

This is why when a wife hears from her husband a topical message such as, "OK, maybe I drove a little too fast, but its no big deal," or "let's not make a federal case out of this," or "why do you make such a big deal out of nothing?" he is conveying to her a relational message that she and her feelings don't matter to him.

Because he isn't aware of the underlying relational communication, but only the topical message, he thought he said, "driving too fast is no big deal." But relationally he said, and she heard, "You are no big deal," or "Your feelings are no big deal." Now there is obviously a huge difference between, "driving too fast is no big deal," and "you or your feelings are no big deal." If the wife then shoots back a statement such as, "You don't love me", or "You don't care," she has just sent him the relational message, "Bad husband. Rejected, disappointment, unacceptable." So he relationally said, "I don't love you," and she relationally responded, "I don't honor or respect you."

Since we have discovered this principle of understanding relational communication, Jan and I frequently joke among ourselves. Since Jan understands my core need for respect, honor and acceptance, she often says to me when I have done something to try to bless or help her, "Good husband." Even though it is sort of a joke, I still appreciate it because it let's me know that she is cognizant of the deep need I have to know that I am acceptable and not a disappointment in her sight.

So in our example above, Tom could not understand why he was such a "bad husband" because he denied his own desire to watch the football game and honored his children's request to take them to the state fair. Likewise, Sue could not understand how she and her feelings could mean so little to Tom as to be excluded from an annual family outing. Both Tom and Sue were focused only on the topical communication and both were blind to the underlying relational messages being sent. Consequently, neither of them could apologize for the relational messages they had sent, and convey the true feelings in their hearts toward each other.

How To Drive Your Husband Away

Let's consider one more example. Cathy had been praying for her husband, Joe, for a couple of years. Joe had committed his life to the Lord several years ago, but had never really grown spiritually or had any great interest in spiritual things. Cathy, on the other hand had grown tremendously in the last couple of years. Since her children were in school during the day and she didn't work outside the home, she had a fair amount of time to pursue spiritual things. Cathy listened to Christian radio most of the day while working around her house and was able to spend a couple of hours in Bible study and prayer almost every day after the kids left for school. She also attended a women's Bible study once a week, a home fellowship group, and church a couple of times a week.

Joe's job as an attorney kept him very busy. He was frequently required to travel out of town and often had to work late into the evening. Cathy had been praying that Joe would get as excited about and committed to the Lord as she was. She wanted him to really become the spiritual head of the home. Frequently, she left interesting CDs for him to hear in his car on the way to work, but he rarely listened to them.

One weekend Cathy convinced Joe to try studying the Bible and praying with her for just ten minutes each morning before work. She was so excited when he agreed. Cathy called up several of her friends on the phone and asked them to pray for Joe on Monday morning.

Cathy was bubbling over with excitement as she and Joe sat down to read the Bible Monday morning. "Well, what part would you like to read?" she inquired.

"I don't know," Joe answered. So Cathy suggested the book that she had been studying in the women's Bible study. Joe agreed. They opened up their Bibles and read the first chapter. Cathy then asked Joe to comment on what the Lord was speaking to him through the passage. Joe was feeling a little uncomfortable, because he was really out of his field and wasn't exactly sure what it meant to have the Lord speak, anyway. He mentioned a couple of things that he saw in the passage. Cathy, in her zeal to expose to Joe the richness and depth of the Bible, then proceeded to expound upon the passage for about ten minutes. Joe was silent.

She then said, "Let's pray now." Joe agreed. Joe had always felt a little uncomfortable praying aloud, but he went ahead and awkwardly muttered a couple sentences asking for wisdom and praying for God's blessing for the day. Cathy then entered into His presence, put on the armor, bound the devil, spoke the Word, released the power, pled the blood, and prayed for the missionaries, all in Jesus' name. When she finished, Joe said he was in a hurry and quickly left for work.

The next morning Joe said that he couldn't pray with her, because he had to be at the office a little early. He continued to make excuses not to meet with her again for prayer and Bible study. Cathy was once again disappointed and hurt that Joe just wasn't interested in spiritual things.

What Cathy had failed to realize was that there was an Ephesians 6:10-12 scheme working in her marriage. Without knowing it, she was conveying to Joe the "bad husband" disrespectful relational message. Her goal was to interest him in spiritual things and to help him assume a role of spiritual leadership in the home. But, instead, through her insensitivity to her husband's need to feel significant and adequate as a husband, Cathy was continually sending him the message that he was a spiritual disappointment and was unacceptable in her sight.

When women are hurt inside and have had their identities damaged by their husbands, frequently they will express such to their husbands in some way. However, often when a husband is hurt and has had his identity damaged by his wife, he won't express it, but rather will withdraw from relationship and just be silent. That is what Joe did. Cathy didn't understand Joe's reaction and interpreted it as his having no interest in spiritual matters.

Actually, Joe had a great interest in spiritual things, but was threatened by Cathy's superior knowledge of the Bible and practice in the language of prayer. Without knowing it, Cathy was constantly wounding her husband and making him feel very foolish around her. There was no way he could compete with her spirituality, and it deeply hurt him to be made to feel so inadequate. Consequently, he simply wouldn't participate with his wife in spiritual things. The more Cathy tried to get Joe to hear this CD, read that book, pray with her, or go to this meeting, the more she unwittingly drove him away from the Lord and from intimacy with her.

Resolution Through Repentance

How is the type of miscommunication that was between Tom and Sue and Joe and Cathy resolved? Once either or both parties begin to become aware of and sensitive to the underlying relational communication messages, this type of conflict is really quite easy to resolve. The first step is to realize that there really is a spiritual battle over the marriage, and that our battle really is not against flesh and blood (Ephesians 6:10-12). "The arms dealer" will use our own blind areas to get us to unwittingly send our spouse a relational message of lack of love or disrespect.

How do I know when I have just unwittingly sent my spouse a wounding relational message? As I mentioned with Joe and Cathy, when most people receive a wounding relational message, they will respond in one of two ways: 1) Fight, or 2) Flight. Some people lash out in anger, while others close up and withdraw. You can immediately tell when the enemy has used you to send a wounding relational message to your spouse by just being aware of your spouse's countenance and voice intonation. When you see or hear your spouse lash out in anger or close up and withdraw seemingly for no reason, you can know that an Ephesians 6:10-12 scheme was just worked against you by the enemy.

Once you realize the scheme, you then have a choice. You can respond by justifying your position and arguing with your marriage partner about the topical issue, or you can acknowledge that you wounded him on a relational level, repent and ask forgiveness. I have found that many people have great difficulty understanding that being right on the topical level has no bearing on resolving a wound on the relational level. For example, Tom might have said, "Why should I ask Sue to forgive me? Forgive me for what, being a good father and blessing my children by

115

taking them to the fair? I have done nothing wrong and she is falsely accusing me." If he were to do this, he would perpetuate the scheme of the devil in his marriage and further destroy relationship and intimacy with Sue.

Or, Cathy could have said, "Why should I apologize to Joe? Apologize for what, loving the Lord with all my heart, and wanting my husband to take his place as the spiritual priest of our home?" If she were to respond this way, she would continue to wound her husband and probably he would continue to close up and withdraw more from her and from the Lord. She would be producing in her marriage relationship exactly the opposite results from those she was desiring.

But I'm Not Wrong

I have found that one of the greatest hindrances for a husband to acknowledge and repent of wounding his wife is that he is convinced he is right and therefore has no need or repentance. It is critical for a husband to understand that he might indeed be right on the topical level, but still have been used to wound his wife on the relational level. This is what was initially preventing Tom from repenting and asking Sue to forgive him for not calling her or including her. He didn't feel that he should be held accountable for something he didn't know and he had no malicious intent in his heart to hurt Sue. Consequently, he was convinced that she was just oversensitive and needed to get over it.

Although this is frequently the main hindrance preventing men from resolving the relational wound, it is not unique to husbands. This same blindness to the relational message and feeling of being right was the same thinking that prevented Cathy from repenting of wounding her husband Joe on the relational level. She felt that she was right to pursue relationship with God with all of her heart and to desire for her husband to do the same and to take his place as the spiritual head of their household.

116

Here is the point: Even though you didn't have any intent in your heart to wound, and you may be right on the topical level, if the enemy has used you to send a negative personal value relational message of lack of love to your wife or of disrespect or dishonor to your husband, you must take responsibility for this, apologize and ask forgiveness.

Blind, Not Evil

I have found that the one of greatest hindrances for a wife to resolve relational wounding with her husband is that she cannot believe that he did not wound her intentionally. Sue had great difficulty believing Tom when he said that it just didn't dawn on him to call her before he took the kids to the fair. When I have suggested to a wife that her husband really didn't intend to wound her, and that he really was blind in this area, she would look at me in disbelief. She would then comment, "No, not possible. No one is that dense, stupid and insensitive. Anyone would know or see …(whatever he didn't do or see.)"

The truth is that any <u>woman</u> would see or know that, but most men would not. Sue honestly had difficulty believing that most husbands when faced with a similar situation would not have thought to call their wives before taking the kids to the state fair. In this case, the truth was that Tom was blind, not evil. He had no malicious intent in his heart toward Sue.

When they receive an unloving, wounding relational message from their husbands, most wives conclude that the husband knew he was hurting her, and that he just didn't care. This then makes him unfeeling, uncaring and probably actually malicious and evil in her mind. It doesn't usually occur to her that this could be an Ephesians 6:11 scheme of the devil, and that her husband may not be evil, but rather may be blind and not be aware that he is hurting her. I believe that considering this possibility would make a huge difference in most marriage relationships.

There is quite a huge difference in relationship between evil and blind. If a man walking down the street runs right into you as you are looking the other way and knocks some sacks of groceries out of your hands, you might initially be quite offended and angry.

Suppose you looked over at him and angrily said, "Why don't you watch where you're going? What's wrong with you, are you blind?"

Then suppose the man answers, "Yes, actually I am blind. I'm sorry. I didn't hear you in front of me. I normally go out with my seeing-eye dog, but unfortunately, he was killed yesterday. Please forgive me for running into you."

This new information regarding the man's blindness and loss of his dog would create an instant paradigm shift for most people. Upon discovering the fact that the reason the man ran into you was that he was blind, not careless or malicious, would motivate most people to instantly forgive him and want to help him rather than be angry with him. If you, as a wife begin to understand that most of the time when your husband wounds you, he is blind, not careless or evil, that will make a great difference. You may want to punish or at least keep at bay a careless or evil man, but wouldn't you want to help a blind man? **Believe me, most husbands are blind, not evil.** Again this is not unique to husbands. In the above example with Joe and Cathy, Cathy was not careless or malicious in her intent toward her husband, Joe. She was just blind and in desperate need of someone to help her see the relational disrespect that she was continually conveying to Joe.

Resolving Relational Miscommunication

Let's now look at seven practical steps to resolve relational wounding messages that damage marriage relationships.

1. Recognize the Ephesians 6:10-12 spiritual battle. When you suddenly get a fight or flight response from your marriage

118

partner, realize that the "arms dealer" just took a shot through you at your spouse. The battle is not against your spouse, but rather against the devil and the kingdom of darkness, whose purpose it is to destroy your marriage.

2. Stop talking on the topical level and ask your spouse how you have just made him <u>feel</u>. The key to understanding the wounding relational message is in understanding the feeling generated.

3. Repeat back to the wounded, sharing partner what you heard him say were the feelings generated. The purpose of this is to verify that you correctly understand how you have made him feel.

4. Take responsibility for sending the relational message (whether it was intentional or not, doesn't matter) and causing the wound by acknowledging that you now understand that you did indeed shoot at your spouse and cause the wound.

5. Ask your spouse to forgive you for wounding him.

6. Convey a true message of love or respect for him from your heart.

7. Let him know that you will use your best efforts not to wound him that way again.

In order to secure the forgiveness of another person, I have found that three things must happen on a heart level. The above-mentioned seven steps to resolve relational wounding are designed to accomplish on a heart level these three things:

A. You must convince the person you have wounded that **you understand how he was wounded** and how he was made to feel of no value.

B. You must convince the person you have wounded that you **take responsibility for wounding him** and that you truly care about his feelings. He must know that it truly grieves you that he was wounded and made to feel worthless.

C. You must convince the person you have wounded that you **will use your best efforts not to wound him** in that way again.

I have found that if you accomplish these three things on a heart level, it is virtually impossible for the one wounded not to forgive you. You can tell if you have really conveyed from the heart these three things, because if you have, there will be an immediate emotional release from the one wounded. His heart will forgive you and the emotional wall between you will be instantly torn down, and you both will know it. If the wall is still there between you, it is an indicator that you haven't yet gotten this job done.

> You can tell if you have really conveyed from the heart these three things, because if you have, there will be an immediate emotional release from the one wounded.

So in the case of Tom and Sue, how would this have worked practically? The moment he heard the disappointed, accusatory tone in Sue's voice on the phone, Tom could have initiated the above seven steps. Let me outline below the type of conversation that Tom needed to initiate with Sue in order to tear down the wall between them and heal the wound inflicted upon Sue. So, the conversation and process might go something like this. Beginning with the phone conversation when Sue called Tom:

"The state fair!" cried Sue in shock and disbelief. "Why did you take the kids to the fair?"

Tom, sensing the "bad husband, you're a failure and a disappointment to me" disrespectful relational message in Sue's voice, would then recognize that they are now no longer talking about the state fair (the topical issue). They are now talking about a relational value message.

His thoughts would then go something like this. "Something just happened. The enemy apparently just used me to send Sue the 'You're worthless, I don't love you, your feelings don't matter' lack of love relational message. I don't know how that happened, but I sense by her tone of voice that it just did." So recognizing the scheme, Tom would terminate talking about the topical issue of justifying why he took the kids to the fair, and initiate conversation on the relational level.

Tom: "Sue, I sense that you are hurt and disappointed that I took the kids to the state fair. Is that true?"

Sue: "I certainly am. How could you take the kids to the fair without even calling me? We always go the fair as a family. Why didn't you call me?"

Tom: Rather than answering her rhetorical question on the topical level, and giving her five logical reasons why he didn't call her first, Tom realizes that he needs to talk about the feelings he has created in her by his oversight, so he says, "I didn't realize it at the time, but I can now see that I made a serious mistake by not communicating with you before I took the kids to the fair. Could you please share with me how I have made you feel by doing that?"

Sue: Still angry, "Yes, you have made me feel like I'm not even a part of this family. Like I don't matter and no one even thinks to include me. I feel like you don't even consider or care about me. Why didn't you call me first?"

Tom: "Honey, I'm so sorry I didn't call you. I didn't realize at the time that by going to the fair without communicating first with you, I would make you feel excluded, like you're not even a part of the family. I can see now that I have made you feel that way and that I have made you feel unloved and not cared for. How else did I make you feel?"

Sue: "Like I don't even matter, and you don't even think about me at all."

Tom: So I made you feel unloved, not a part of the family, not cared for and like you don't matter and I never think about you at all. Is that right?"

Sue: "Yes, that's exactly right. Why would you do that?"

Tom: "Honey, at the time, I was just focused on meeting the needs of the kids. You're right, I wasn't thinking about your feelings. I now understand that I was wrong and that I hurt you deeply. I love you, and the last thing I would ever want to do is hurt you or make you feel like I don't care, or don't love you. But I can see that I have done just that. It deeply grieves me to know that I have made you feel excluded, not a part of our family and like I don't think of or care about you. Would you please forgive me for being so insensitive and inconsiderate toward you?"

Sue: "Yes, I forgive you."

Tom: "I really do love you, and your feelings are important to me. Please pray for me to be more aware of your feelings in the future. I really do want God to change me in that area. I know it can be a blind spot for me and I need your help and God's help to change. Would you please pray for me?"

Sue: "Yes, Tom I will. I realize that you don't always see what's important to me. I was also wrong to snap at you and accuse you the way I just did. Would you please forgive me? I now know you were just trying to do something nice for the kids."

Tom: "Yes, I forgive you. What time do you think you'll be home tonight? Let's spend some more time talking, and I'd like to pray together."

Sue: "OK, that would be great. I should be home about seven. See you then. I love you."

Tom: "Thank you. I love you. See you tonight."

If the conversation would have gone this way, it would have resulted in a totally different outcome than the emotional wall that remained between Tom and Sue for almost two weeks until this process finally did take place.

In the situation with Joe and Cathy, the moment Joe closed up and withdrew, it should have been an indicator to Cathy that an Ephesians 6:10-12 scheme was working against their marriage. She also could have solved it by humbling herself and asking Joe if he would be willing to share with her how she was making him feel. She then could have repented of sending him the "bad husband, you are not what I want or need" relational message.

Had Cathy done this, she could have begun to melt the hardness in her husband's heart and restore the emotional intimacy of their relationship together. She would have released her husband to truly pursue his role as the spiritual head of his home, secure in the respect and honor of his wife, without his personal identity being at stake. However, the reason that Cathy had not repented and asked her husband's forgiveness was because she was convinced that she was right on the topical issue. She thought that the problem was that her husband was just unspiritual and didn't want to know the Lord. She was blind to her own sin of pride and of dishonoring her husband and constantly, through her attitude, devaluing his identity. Consequently, the distance between them continued to grow greater and greater.

If Any Two of You Agree on Earth

One last critical reason for us to work on resolving relational wounding is that these wounds prevent a married couple from coming into agreement with each other regarding key issues in their family and life. It would seem from scripture that when we, as husbands and wives, are in disagreement with each other, we block the Father from working through us in that particular area of life. Jesus said:

*"Again I say to you, **that if two of you agree on earth** about anything that they may ask, it shall be done for them by My Father Who is in heaven"* (Matthew 18:19).

Obviously, the converse is also true. "If any two of you disagree about anything that they may ask, it shall not be done for them by my Father Who is in heaven." So you can see that the Father in heaven is blocked from moving on your behalf often due to disagreement in your marriage. I believe that it is a prime objective of the kingdom of darkness to keep a husband and wife at all costs from coming into agreement with each other. The devil knows the power and synergy that are generated when you as a couple come into agreement and pray. He knows that you release the Father in heaven to do what you have prayed when you are in agreement, so he works very hard through relational miscommunication and wounding to make certain that this does not happen.

To learn and experience more on this topic, you may want to consider attending an 8-week Family Foundations *Communication in Marriage* Course. This is a small group course designed to help couples learn through practical experience how to discern and implement healthy relational communication. For more information you may wish to access the Internet site www.familyfoundations.com

Reflection

1. The arms dealer will always work in the hidden place to set you up to wound your spouse without knowing it.

2. When conflict with your spouse is initiated, know that your spouse is not your enemy, and you have just been set up to shoot at each other by the arms dealer.

3. Become aware of both the topical and relational levels of communication.

4. Recognize that husbands tend to perceive value through the receipt of respect and wives tend to perceive value through the receipt of love.

5. To convey respect is to send your husband the "good husband" message. He needs to know that he is accepted, adequate, and significant in your sight.

6. To convey love means to send your wife the "your feelings matter and you are high priority to me" message. She needs to know that you understand and care how she feels and that her feelings are a big deal to you.

7. Let closing up and withdrawing, or lashing out in anger be an indicator to you that you just sent a wounding relational message to your spouse and you need to switch off of the topical level and deal with the relational message.

8. Resolution of relational miscommunication comes through becoming aware of the relational message sent. Healing and restoration come through repenting and asking forgiveness for generating the hurtful feeling in your spouse.

9. Your spouse will automatically forgive you from the heart if you accomplish the following three things.

   a. You must convince your spouse whom you have wounded that you understand how he was wounded and how he was made to feel of no value.

   b. You must convince your spouse whom you have wounded that you take responsibility for wounding him and that you truly care about his feelings. He must know that it truly grieves you that he was wounded and made to feel worthless.

   c. You must convince your spouse whom you have wounded that you will use your best efforts not to wound him in that way again.

10. Agreement in prayer between a husband and wife releases the hand of God to move on their behalf.

Resources

[1] *An Ancient Paths Seminar*: Empowering Relationships. See Appendix for details and go to www.familyfoundations.com for schedule of upcoming events.

⊙ [1] Communication in Marriage Course—*Renewing the Bond of Love* (See Appendix for details.)

🎧 Supernatural Relationships

📖 You Don't Have to Be Wrong to Repent

c h a p t e r   7

Transparency
and Intimacy

As Jan and I have ministered to and counseled many married couples, a common theme expressed, is that they have lost the feeling of romantic love for each other. I have found that the feeling of romantic love can be directly correlated with the degree of intimacy. Many times when we use the word "intimacy," people are primarily thinking about sexual relationship. While that may be included within the context of intimacy, I am talking here primarily about deep communion of heart and spirit between a husband and wife.

The feeling of romantic love is not a commodity that I either have or don't have. This feeling is actually just a barometer of the amount and depth of intimate communication that is taking place between husband and wife. So when I hear someone say, "I just don't love him (or her) any more," I know that they have not lost some commodity called "love," but rather that they have lost the ability to entertain much intimate communication with each other. When intimate spiritual and emotional communication is restored, usually the feeling of romantic love is also restored right along with it.

So the feeling of romantic love can be likened much more to a bank account, the balance of which goes up or down depending upon deposits or withdrawals, rather than to a commodity I have or don't have. I have found that intimate communication on a heart level is a key to making large bank deposits in your spouse's romantic feeling account. The way many couples "fell in love" in the first place was through sharing with each other on a heart-level their dreams, hopes, aspirations, fears, disappointments, and discouragements. However, after they got married, the flea nature of each took over, and whenever one tried to share again on this level, the other sent the relational message of lack of love or disrespect. This coupled with the scheme of the enemy and relational miscommunication discussed in the last chapter then effectively curtailed or entirely shut down intimate communication on a heart level for most couples. When this has happened, the romantic love feeling account has declined toward zero or below.

Transparency Is The Key To Intimacy

"Therefore a man shall leave his father and mother and be joined to his wife, and they shall become one flesh. And they were both naked, the man and his wife, and were not ashamed" (Genesis 2:24-25).

Many people are familiar with this scripture passage but have not really thought through its true meaning. The first sentence is obviously talking about the fact that God intended for a married couple to become one. However, I think that the second sentence in verse 25 gives us a key as to how this is to happen. We are told that the first husband and wife were naked and not ashamed.

So, what does naked really mean? I don't believe that the primary meaning of "naked and unashamed" is that they were prancing about the garden wearing no clothing. This passage is talking about the fact that they were communicating with each other on a very deep, intimate level. Both of them were open and transparent before each other in all parts of their being, spirit, mind, emotions, and body. I believe that the word "naked" is referring to the fact that they had nothing within themselves to hide from each other.

Since intimacy is a primary key to the feeling of romantic love, and "nakedness" or transparency is the key to intimacy, it is quite critical for us as married couples to learn to have regular times of transparent and intimate communication.

A good saying I have heard many times that may help you to further understand the concept of intimacy is this. Intimacy is an invitation for you to **INTO ME SEE**. Intimacy implies that I am giving you the privilege of looking into the depths of my heart, and I am willing to expose to you whatever is there. This definition then implies a totally transparent, "naked" relationship, with nothing covered and nothing hidden.

> Intimacy implies that I am giving you the privilege of looking into the depths of my heart, and I am willing to expose to you whatever is there.

Verse 25 tells us that the first couple was not only naked and transparent before each other, but that they were also not ashamed. Shame implies a deep fear of discovery of things about me that I don't want you to know. Things that I don't like about myself, or things that I know are wrong. So when I have such things present in my life, if covenant is not in place in a marriage then I may be greatly afraid that if you truly find out about me those ugly things I know about myself, you may abandon me. This fear will cause me to walk in shame and hide those things from my spouse. When this is the case, there can be very little intimacy.

So we see that intimacy is dependent upon transparency, and transparency is dependent upon covenant trust. If I am fearful that my wife will leave me if I really share with her the ugly areas of my soul, past or present behavior, then I am compelled by that very powerful fear and shame to hide and not disclose those areas of my life. On the other hand, if I know that my wife is unconditionally committed to our marriage in covenant, then I may be willing to take the risk to share with her those areas of my life. This is why we have spent several chapters in the beginning and end of this book discussing the re-establishment of the value of covenant in marriage.

In a marriage, when we keep things hidden from each other, it destroys intimacy. Although my marriage partner may not know all the details, he will know that something is keeping a wall between us. I think that many times people buy into the deception that it is better not to share things that might hurt a spouse. The thinking is, "if he doesn't know about it, then he won't be hurt by it." It may be true that your spouse doesn't know the detail, but hidden things always destroy intimacy. Furthermore, when there are hidden areas of your life, then you are always subject to the blackmail of the devil. In the back of your mind there is always the thought that this ugly thing may be exposed at some inopportune time.

Of course the problem with hidden things is that they don't remain hidden forever. I remember hearing a wise man once say regarding hidden things, that we all have our choice of humility or humiliation. The definitions given were something like these.

Humility: A wise person confessing his true behavior and character to God and those who love him.

Humiliation: A foolish person who has hidden his shameful behavior or character being exposed publicly for all to see.

Not only in marriage, but also in many other areas of life, whenever I have felt that blackmailing pressure of the enemy with the thought, "You have done this wrong, or lied to this person and covered it or sinned in this area and I will expose you," I have always said, "Then I'll expose it first." Each time that I have exposed to Jan or to others whom I trust, things I have been motivated to try to cover, there was always a fear that I would be rejected and lose credibility. Each time, it was difficult to do, but each time just the opposite of what I had feared actually took place. When I opened and confessed hidden areas, I gained favor and credibility with Jan and others rather than lost it.

Whoever Loses His Life Will Save It

I remember one of the first times I learned this lesson in my marriage. This event took place back in the earlier days of our marriage before we had learned much about relational communication messages. I was doing some volunteer counseling at our church. Jan asked what time I would be back home. I told her that my last appointment was at 7:00 PM and should finish at 8:00. It would take me about 10 minutes to gather my things and leave, about 30 minutes to drive home, so I should be there about 8:40.

> When I opened and confessed hidden areas I gained favor and credibility with Jan and others rather than lost it.

After my last appointment, as I was passing through the foyer of the church, I began to converse with another one of the volunteer counselors who had been there that day. She mentioned to me a scripture verse about which she had been thinking. That triggered another thought I had been thinking. We then got into a very interesting discussion about a biblical topic pertinent to ministering to people. Eight thirty came and went. Then nine o'clock, nine thirty and it was

131

approaching ten o'clock. I finally told her, "I have to go," and ran out to my car and started home.

This time was before the days of cell phones, so I couldn't call Jan and tell her I was late. On the way home I continued thinking about the things I had just learned through our conversation. Suddenly, I was rudely interrupted by a very disturbing thought about what I would tell Jan as to why I was coming home two hours later than I had said. My immediate reaction was to want to hide the truth and tell her a lie.

I thought, "If I tell her the truth, it will hurt her and she will be angry with me." I thought that she would be angry for at least two reasons. The first was that I had dishonored my time commitment to her again. This was not the first time that I had come home much later than I had said. Unfortunately, there had been no emergency reason for my tardiness. I had simply chosen to continue a conversation that was interesting to me. Secondly, because Jan and I had relationally wounded each other, we were not talking together about deep spiritual truth, but yet I had just chosen to spend two hours doing so with someone else.

As I pondered telling Jan that I had simply chosen to spend the last two hours conversing with someone instead of coming home, there was a powerful compelling motivation to cover that fact and tell her something like, "When I came out of my last appointment there was a ministry situation going on in the foyer of the church, and I was needed. We had a very powerful time with the Lord in which we saw several people physically healed as we prayed, two marriages were saved, seven others committed their lives to Christ, and I left to come home as quickly as I could. I just couldn't leave until we were finished." That sounded like a much better story. The thought also occurred to me, "She will never know what really happened. Why does it matter anyway? The details are not important as to why I was late."

Just at that moment, the Holy Spirit brought to my remembrance another scripture verse, *"For whoever desires to save his own life will lose it, but whoever loses his life for My sake and the gospel's will save it"* (Mark 8:35). I sensed the Holy Spirit say to me, "By hiding the truth and concocting your own false story, you are simply attempting to save your own life. If you do so, you will lose the very thing you are trying to save." Another string of thoughts from God also then came directly to my mind. "Short-term fixes (such as hiding truth) are always the seed of long term destruction. You have your choice of humility or humiliation, as you will not escape the consequences of sowing and reaping. Your only choice is short-term death to self by telling Jan the truth, leading to long-term trust and life in your marriage, or short-term life by lying to Jan, leading to long-term distrust and destruction in your marriage."

> Whenever one spouse chooses to hide even small things within a marriage, it sets up a pattern of lying, hiding, and distrust in that marriage.

Whenever one spouse chooses to hide even small things within a marriage, it sets up a pattern of lying, hiding, and distrust in that marriage. Even though the other partner may not know exactly what happened, he will know that there is something between you in the marriage. Such hidden things do not permit the one hiding from completely opening his life to transparency and thus intimacy. Some people have lived this lifestyle for so long that they think living with hidden secrets is normal in a marriage, and cannot even imagine a life of true transparency with a spouse.

On the way home that evening, I had a major battle with the Lord about whether I really should tell Jan the complete truth about why I was late. Again, my own fleadom was greatly exposed that evening. I could see that because I was not a battery looking to God to energize and fill me, I was a flea looking to Jan to fill and energize me. I was afraid that if I told her the truth she would be angry with me and not meet my needs for emotional life and peace. I finally realized that I had to choose whether I would continue to live as a flea and seek to save my own emotional life first short-term, or whether I would choose to be a free man who would choose to act in Jan's best interest and to sow seeds of trust instead of distrust into my marriage.

When I arrived home, as I came in I told Jan, "I would like to tell you some long story as to why I am late. However, the truth of the matter is that I simply chose to spend two hours talking to Sally (not her real name) in the church foyer instead of honoring my time commitment to you. I now realize that I was wrong to do so, and that I was selfish and just chose to do what I wanted to do when I wanted to do it, instead of considering the commitment I made to you to be home at 8:40. I really do want to change in that area. Will you please forgive me and pray for me to let God change me?"

I was then shocked by Jan's response. Rather than being angry, she forgave me. We then talked a lot more and prayed together that evening. I'll never forget one of the things Jan told me that evening. **She said, "I think I could handle almost anything you do wrong. What I cannot handle is if you lie to me about it.** When you lie or hide truth, you cut me out of your life. The betrayal of lying and deception hurts me far more than anything wrong you could ever do." Before that evening, I don't think I really understood the deep feeling of betrayal when one is deceived or lied to.

In this circumstance, what the devil meant for evil to damage and wound our marriage turned out to strengthen and deepen our marriage. We talked that evening on a deeper, more intimate level than we had in many years. Truth and transparency always opens the door to intimacy. Since that time, neither Jan nor I have ever carried anything hidden between us that the devil could use to blackmail us or damage our intimacy.

I know that when some people read this, they will think, "Yeah, but you don't know what I have done. It is a little worse than talking to someone in a church and coming home two hours late." I realize that some people have thought, said, or done some pretty terrible and betraying things, many of which may have been hidden for years. However, I know that hiding things in a marriage always destroys the potential for intimacy and the feeling of romantic love. Certainly the disclosure of adultery, or other sexually illicit relationships can be very traumatic. If you are convicted now that there are such hidden things in your life that have never been disclosed, I recommend that you seek some godly counsel regarding the timing and way you should go about sharing that part of your life with your spouse. However, not sharing it will for sure hinder your intimacy and will keep a wall between you.

Jan and I have some good friends, Bob and Audrey Meisner, who have had to walk through this situation. After 19 years of marriage, Audrey committed adultery. At first, she thought of just terminating the adulterous relationship and hiding her sin. However, she knew that if she did so, she would always carry the guilt, and never be clean before God. Furthermore, even though her husband, Bob, may not have known what had happened, he would know that there was a wall between them and their intimacy was not the same. As a result of this knowledge, Audrey chose humility and freedom rather than humiliation and fleadom.

Needless to say, there was tremendous short-term emotional death for both Bob and Audrey with the disclosure of the adultery, but it brought long-term life into their marriage. Bob and Audrey have written a book about their journey through this experience called, *Marriage Under Cover*[1]. I highly recommend this book for any couple. However, if you have a serious area of your

[1] Meisner, Bob and Audrey, *Marriage Under Cover*, Milestones International Publishers, Huntsville, AL, 2005

life that has never been disclosed to your spouse, the Mesiner's book would be a great resource for you. In order to restore or establish intimacy, I highly recommend that you disclose any still hidden areas of your life to your spouse and then establish a lifestyle of openness and transparency, which will result in increased intimacy.

Danger of Soulical (Emotional) Adultery

We talked earlier about the feeling of romantic love being like a bank account balance, rather than a commodity one has or does not have. When the romantic feeling balance is near or below zero, there is a potential danger in that marriage for one or both partners to inadvertently or purposefully open an account in their heart toward another person. If someone at work, church, or some other setting begins to listen to me without judgment or running commentary on why my thoughts or feelings are wrong, then I may choose to share more from my heart with that person. I call this situation "soulical adultery," (emotional adultery in the soul).

If I continue this sharing from the heart, without realizing it, I have opened an account in my heart toward this other person. Unknowingly, I am now headed down the track toward soulical adultery, and eventually physical adultery. If I continue this process, the account balance may grow to the point that I suddenly notice I am experiencing romantic or sexual feelings toward this other person to whom I am not married. At this point, I am shocked, as I, myself thought this was just an innocent friendship. Not understanding this sowing and reaping process is how many adulterous affairs begin. In reality, intimate communication is taking place with this other person on a level that it is not taking place with a spouse, and this is meeting a deep need inside.

A person in such relationship, not understanding this process may then conclude, "I just don't love my spouse any more, but I have 'fallen in love' with this other person." No, that is a deception. The truth is that you simply stopped communicating in intimacy with your wife or husband and began doing so with this other person. Sowing and reaping has dictated that the balance in your romantic love feeling account toward your spouse depleted, while the balance in your heart account, that you didn't even know you had opened toward the other person, has steadily increased. The feeling of romantic love then, is not mystical or magical, but rather just plain and simple sowing and reaping.

So, the key to affair-proofing your marriage is to not just try to stop the potential feelings toward other people, but rather to keep an open channel of regular, intimate communication with your spouse. When the feeling of romantic love in your heart toward your spouse is high due to regular intimate communication between you, there is very little motivation or temptation to begin that process of sharing from the heart with others.

Perhaps you can easily see the potential for a soulical adultery relationship to develop for pastors, business leaders, counselors and people in helping professions, who are much in demand and very busy. Because they live their lives with no margins, and are so busy giving out to everyone else, these leaders frequently have no more time or energy to sow into intimate communication with their own spouse when they arrive home. Then when a personal assistant, coworker, or friend sees the stress and pressure that the leader is under, she innocently makes opportunity for that leader to begin to talk and unload some of the pressure on a heart level.

Since the pastor or leader is not making time for intimate conversation at home, he may be picking up criticism, disrespect, and rejection from his wife, while his assistant coworker, or friend is conveying to him a message of acceptance, honor and respect. Naturally he will tend to gravitate toward the accepting, pleasant conversation with the coworker, and avoid the critical, unpleasant, or at best, neutral conversation with his wife. This, then is another hidden Ephesians 6:10-12 scheme of the devil working in his life, designed to destroy his marriage and lead him into soulical adultery, and ultimately an extramarital affair. I used the example here of a man in ministry or business, but this scenario is not unique to men, and may equally apply to a woman in such a position.

Let me give you a very simple three-question test to determine if you are in danger and have an emotional account open toward another person right now.

1) When you receive exciting or good news, is there someone whom you would rather call or share that information with first ahead of your spouse?

2) Is there another person of the opposite sex with whom you are regularly talking on a much deeper spiritual and/or emotional level (hopes, dreams, future plans, aspirations, insights, fears, frustrations, pain) than you are with your spouse?

3) Is it easier or more pleasant to talk with this other person than with your spouse? Are you sharing your marital frustrations with this person?

If the answer to any of these questions is yes, you are probably in soulical adultery right now. To remedy this, I would suggest closing the emotional account in your heart with that other person, and immediately stop sharing with him any feelings or heart-level communication. If the relationship has developed to the point of battling romantic or sexual feelings toward that person, it is critical that you immediately terminate the relationship and have no further contact with that person.

Furthermore, it is critical to reopen the channels of intimate communication with your spouse. This process may be very difficult to do on your own. I would highly suggest that you attend an FFI *Ancient Paths Seminar*, and seek out a counselor or mentor couple to help you walk through this process. If you don't know anyone who can help you, I suggest you contact the National Association of Marriage Enhancement (NAME)[2] organization for suggestions of people who might be able to help you in your local area.

Shame Causes Us To Hide

Shame is a very potent force that compels us to want to hide things about ourselves that are wrong, ugly, or things we don't like. Apostle Paul talks about dealing with these things in the following scripture passage:

*"But we have **renounced the hidden things of shame**, not walking in craftiness nor handling the word of God deceitfully, but by manifestation of truth commending ourselves to every man's conscience in the sight of God. But even if our gospel is veiled, it is veiled for those who are perishing, whose minds the god of this age has blinded, who do not believe, lest the light of the gospel of the glory of Christ, who is the image of God should shine on them. For we do not preach ourselves, but Christ Jesus the Lord, and ourselves as your bondservants for Jesus' sake. For it is God Who commanded light to shine out of darkness, who has shone in our hearts to give the light of the knowledge of the glory of god in the face of Jesus Christ. But we have this treasure in earthen vessels, that the excellence of the power may be of God and not of us"* (II Corinthians 4:2-7).

In this passage, Paul instructs us to renounce those things that we have hidden as a result of shame. What does renounce mean? It means things such as to disown, put aside, put off. It is critical for us to understand that just as hidden things destroy intimacy in a marriage, hidden things also destroy intimacy with God. Obviously, nothing is really hidden from God, since He sees it all. But, if I have an area of wrongdoing in my life that I have never openly confessed to God and asked for forgiveness, then that area will hinder my intimacy with Him and my ability to come to Him with a clear conscience.

---

[2] For more information go to the Internet site: www.nameonline.net

Besides destroying intimacy with God and a spouse, there are a couple of other consequences talked about in this passage. The first is that when we have hidden areas in our lives, we then tend to walk in craftiness. In this sense, craftiness means deceitfulness and/or treachery. Once I have chosen to hide, lie or deceive, I frequently then have to tell more lies to cover the first one. So, I begin to live a lifestyle of deceit and craftiness.

Secondly, I will begin to handle the word of God deceitfully. I believe that this has a couple of meanings. The first is that I may begin to distort the true and clear meaning of the Bible to suit the lifestyle I have chosen. This means that one's interpretation of scripture is determined by one's morality and lifestyle, rather than one's morality and lifestyle being determined by scripture. I have frequently discovered that when I run into someone who is very argumentative about the Bible, and has chosen interpretations that are directly contrary to what is clearly stated in scripture, it has later been exposed that this person had hidden aspects of his life that were supported by such interpretations.

Another detrimental consequence of hiding is that there is incongruity between that which is spoken or taught and that which is lived. If there is a hidden area in the life of someone who ministers the word of God, then not only is the word of God being handled deceitfully, but the gospel is then veiled to others. People sitting under the preaching or teaching of that person are confused. They hear the minister speaking one thing from the word of God, but projecting something entirely different from his spirit. This, then causes confusion in the hearts of the hearers, and the gospel becomes veiled.

Jan and I have found that it is important for couples who are pastors or people who publicly teach the word of God in some capacity to understand that the state of their own unity and marital relationship will affect the ministry of the word of God to others. I first learned this through Dave and Maxine Broom[3], precious friends of ours, and a ministry couple from Harare, Zimbabwe in Africa. Several times I have heard Dave and Maxine share the following story.

Disunity Pollutes Others

Many years ago Dave and Maxine made an agreement with each other before the Lord that they would never preach or teach the word of God publicly with unresolved strife between them in their marriage. The reason for this is that they understood from Second Corinthians chapter four that to do so, they would be handling the word of God deceitfully, rather than in truth and integrity. They had been conducting some ministry training in a particular church in the U.K. over the weekend and then were to speak in the Sunday morning service of this same church.

However, in a social function on the Saturday evening before the day they were to speak in the church, Dave and Maxine had a knock-down-drag-out fight that created deep strife between them. When they got back to their room they attempted to resolve the issue, but without success. Both went to bed angry with each other. When they woke up in the morning, they had more discussion about this issue, but by the time they needed to leave for the church service, they were still in strife with each other and the issue was unresolved.

It was a very difficult situation since the church had heavily advertised for several months in advance that they were having special international guest speakers at the service that morning. Consequently, the church was full, with both regular members and visitors who had come specially to hear the Brooms. How-

---

[3] Broom, Dave & Maxine, Renewal Ministries, *Family Dynamics Courses on CD & DVD,* www.renewalmin.org

ever, Dave and Maxine had made a commitment before the Lord, which they felt they must honor.

So, when it came time to introduce their guest ministers, the pastor got up and gave a very warm welcome and introduction and said, "And all the way from Zimbabwe, Africa we have to speak to us today, Dave and Maxine Broom." At that, Dave got up and announced to the congregation, "Unfortunately, you won't be hearing from Dave and Maxine Broom this morning. You see, years ago we made an agreement before the Lord that we would never publicly preach or teach when we have unresolved issues between us as a married couple. This morning, Maxi and I still have a huge unresolved issue causing strife and anger between us, and all I know to do is to share that with you, and ask if your pastor and elders would come and pray for God to help us and to heal our hearts toward one another."

The pastor and elders then came. Just before they began to pray, one of the elders who had frequently preached in the church said, "I have something that I would like to confess. I have several times recently done in this very pulpit what Dave and Maxine were unwilling to do here today. I have stood and preached when my wife and I were in severe disharmony and strife and defiled this congregation with our unresolved mess. I want to ask you in this congregation to forgive me for doing so." Many people then responded by voicing their forgiveness.

The pastor and leaders then began to pray for Dave and Maxine. Dave then told us that as he and Maxine were receiving prayer, they heard some commotion out in the congregation. When he looked up, 90% of the people were no longer in their seats, but rather were on their knees or faces on the floor weeping and praying. He said that for the next hour or so there was a tremendous move of the Holy Spirit across the entire group in repentance and life-changing experiences with the Lord for many people. It was interesting that not one verse of scripture was read and not one word preached or taught, and yet there was a profound impact upon the entire congregation that morning.

After the service, Dave was asking the Lord why there had been such a powerful move of the Holy Spirit in that church that morning. He heard the Father say, "Son, I will always build on a foundation of truth." This Dave interpreted to mean, "When you refused to bow to potential pressure to minister while not in integrity in your marriage, but rather to speak the truth even though it was uncomfortable to you and perhaps a potential disappointment to the people, that is what opened the door for My Spirit to move in the hearts of the people."

So Dave and Maxine found that instead of hiding and covering the fact that they were in the midst of a huge argument with each other that was very emotional and not yet resolved, when they disclosed that truth, they gained favor and credibility with the people in the church, rather than lost it. This, of course, is a principle that is not only true in marriage, but is also true in business, in government, in church or in any setting.

The Gospel is Veiled

The last part of this passage in Second Corinthians chapter four tells us that we are earthen vessels filled with the glory of Christ. The picture I get from this is that of translucent vessels. The light is inside, but it must show through the translucent vessel in order for anyone to see it. Unfortunately, if the light inside me is bright, as it shines, it will expose any flaws or imperfections in the vessel through which it is shining.

The primary scheme of the devil in this case is to point out to me any and all flaws in me, the vessel, and get me to focus on, and become very self-conscious and fearful of rejection by others due to exposure of those flaws and imperfections. When this happens, I will then do everything I can to cover the vessel so that no one can see the imperfections. When I cover the vessel, I also cloak the light inside so that no one can see it either. The devil can't stop the light of Christ from shining out through me, so his only strategy is to get me to purposefully cover and hide the vessel and the light with it so that the light cannot be seen by or help anyone else.

Walking on Eggshells

In addition to this, when there is a lack of transparency in marriage, it frequently causes couples to feel like they are walking on eggshells around each other. When one or both marriage partners are retaining hidden areas in their lives, there is a constant underlying fear of exposure. The hider then will use many various defense mechanisms to keep from being exposed. Some of the common tactics used to keep one's spouse at bay are anger, criticism, humor and joking, closing up and withdrawing.

For example, if asked, "Why did you come home two hours late?" the one who is hiding may respond in anger, "It's none of your business. You're not my mother. I'll come home when I please." Anger usually effectively shuts down communication and any further questioning about a hidden area. The other tactics mentioned are also used just as effectively to do the same thing.

As you have been reading this chapter, if there have come to your mind things in your life that have been hidden from your spouse, I encourage you to plan to make a time when you can sit down together and you can disclose these things to him.

Face To Face Rather Than Side By Side

We talked in the beginning of this book about four different stages of marriage: two drowning people, two fleas, two independent swimmers and finally two people in a canoe headed for a destination. It is not possible to move to the fourth stage of marriage, paddling the canoe together, without having significant intimacy with each other. Most people stop in the development of their marriage at the independent swimmer stage. This stage is best pictured by two people going through life side by side, but never face to face. Face to face interaction requires trust and intimacy. Many times when I have asked a married couple to face each other and look into each other's eyes, they cannot sustain direct eye contact for more than a few seconds. Often they begin to laugh, or look down or turn away. Intimacy is potentially intimidating if a couple is not used to the regular experience.

I would like to give you two exercises that will help you build intimate conversation as a couple. One is a prayer exercise, while the other is a conversation exercise. You may have heard the statistic that about one in every two couples in North America divorce. You may not have heard, however, the following information. About one in every two couples who go to church divorce. About one in every two couples who regularly read the Bible divorce. But only one in over 1,100 couples who have a regular habit of praying together daily divorce. So apparently praying together is a key divorce prevention mechanism.

> Praying together is a key divorce prevention mechanism.

We have learned from our friends Bob and Audrey Meisner a particular way of praying face to face, rather than side to side that helps to build intimacy in the marriage. Bob and Audrey have taught thousands of couples around the world how to practice this habit daily.

Here's how it works. As a couple you sit directly facing each other. Look directly into each other's eyes. (The eyes are the windows of the soul.) You will then pray to God while looking into your spouse's eyes. (Yes, God can hear you even if you have your eyes open.) The prayer will include three components: 1) Repentance; 2) Thanksgiving; 3) Blessing.

I believe that it is appropriate for the husband to begin first to pray through these three areas. When he has finished, then the wife will pray the same for the husband. Let me outline how to pray each area.

A. **Repentance:** You will first ask God to remind you of any unconfessed areas in which you have been unloving or disrespectful toward your spouse since the last time you prayed. You simply want to ask the Lord to reveal any instances in which you have sinned against or wounded your spouse with which you have not yet dealt. If or when something comes to your mind, you will then, still looking into your wife's/husband's eyes, confess to him what has come to your mind and ask him to forgive you. Example: "Sue please forgive me for not considering your feelings and not calling you in advance about going with the kids to the state fair this afternoon."

B. **Thanksgiving:** While still looking into your wife's/husband's eyes, you will speak several sentences to God, thanking Him for those qualities in your spouse. Example: "Father, thank you so much for Jan. I thank you that she is so beautiful to look at this morning. Thank you that she loves You with all her heart and that she is a diligent seeker of You, whom you strongly reward. Thank you that she is a wonderful mother and makes our home a refuge and a place of peace."

C. **Blessing:** While still looking into your wife's/husband's eyes, you will speak several sentences of blessing over your spouse. Example: "Father, I want to pray your blessing over Tom today. I bless Tom with the mind of Christ and your wisdom in all the business decisions he has to make today. Father, I declare Your divine favor over Tom with all of his creditors, vendors and employees this week. I bless him with physical health, inner peace, and may Your word dwell richly in Tom all day today, in the name of Jesus, the Messiah. Amen."

I encourage you to find a regular time every day when you can pray with and for each other in this way. As you can see, this prayer model can be accomplished in just a few minutes. You don't need to find an hour to do this, but only five minutes. If you establish this as a habit, I believe that you will make it very hard for the devil to work very many schemes against you, and you will make it very hard for his schemes to prosper for long in your marriage. In addition, you will significantly increase the intimacy between you.

Ask Each Other the Real Questions

The second exercise I would like to encourage you to practice is one designed to deepen your intimacy in conversation with each other. We have designed some questions that I have come to call "THE REAL QUESTIONS." I call them this because many married couples never "get real" with each other. They don't actually talk about feelings because it is too likely to lead to disagreements and strife. However, if we never talk about feelings, then we never establish intimacy. So we have outlined a process below and a list of 10 "Real Questions."

> If we never talk about feelings, then we never establish intimacy.

If you are in Stage 1 or 2 of your marriage, you may find this second exercise too difficult to accomplish alone. If you try it and it leads to serious conflict, I would suggest only pursuing it in the presence of your counselor or mentor couple. Let them help lead you through the process and help you resolve the resulting conflict.

Here is how the process works. Again, I would suggest that the husband initiate the process by asking his wife to honestly answer the first three questions. After she has done so, reverse the roles and the wife will ask the husband to honestly answer the first three questions. Then repeat this process with the next three questions, until you have asked all ten. You may take several sessions to get through all of the questions. So here is the process.

The goal of this process is to listen to and understand <u>the feelings</u> of your spouse, not to defend, justify, criticize, or withdraw. Therefore, these are the ground rules.

A. One partner at a time will share the real answer to one question at a time.

B. The listening partner may not interrupt or offer commentary.

C. When the sharing partner has finished, the listening partner will repeat back to the sharing partner what the sharing partner has said.

D. The sharing partner will verify whether the listening partner has understood or not. If not, repeat steps A—D.

E. The listening partner will now respond (still no defending, justifying, criticizing, or withdrawing). If the answer to the question was positive, the listening partner will say, "Thank you." If the answer to the question was negative, the listening partner may choose to ask for forgiveness. The listening partner may then want to initiate prayer together to ask for God's help to change this area of his life.

Husband you are to start. The goal is for you to understand what your wife's experience and feeling truly is in living with you. You want to know: **"Honestly, what kind of a man am I to live with?"** Her answer to each question should be one of the following:

All of the time,

Most of the time,

Rarely, or

Never.

Questions For Your Wife

1. Do you feel invited to share your heart with me? Would you feel safe and confident in my response to your true feelings? This means you don't fear my response, and I don't make you feel unsafe to share your inner thoughts with me?

2. Do you feel needed by me, or do I make you feel that I am self-sufficient and I don't really need you spiritually, emotionally, or sexually?

3. Do I use anger, humiliation or shutting down (fleaing) to keep you from touching things inside me that might hurt expose, or embarrass me?

4. Do I make you feel like I don't value your opinions and feelings; that I think your opinions are foolish and I don't really care about your feelings?

5. Do you feel pursued by me? Do I make you feel beautiful and worth fighting for?

6. Do I make you feel used, not beautiful, or foolish in my sight?

7. Has our marriage turned out to be what you had always hoped for when we first got married?

8. Do you look forward to sexual relationship with me?

9. Do you look forward to spending time alone with me?

10. Do you find excuses to be busy with work, other people or projects to avoid spending time with me?

Now it is the wife's turn. The goal again is for you to understand what your husband's experience and feeling truly is in living with you. You want to know: **"Honestly, what kind of a woman am I to live with?"** His answer to each question should be one of the following:

All of the time,

Most of the time,

Rarely, or

Never.

Questions For Your Husband

1. Do you feel invited to share your heart with me? Would you feel safe and confident in my response to your true feelings? This means you don't fear my response, and I don't make you feel unsafe to share your inner thoughts with me?

2. Do you feel needed by me, or do I make you feel that I am self-sufficient and I don't really need you spiritually, emotionally, or sexually.

3. Do I use anger, humiliation, or shutting down (fleaing) to keep you from touching things inside me that might hurt expose or embarrass me?

4. Do I make you feel like I don't value your decisions and that I think that I would be a much better head of the house than you are?

5. Do I make you feel like a real man, someone I respect and greatly look up to?

6. Do I make you feel emasculated, unspiritual, incompetent, or like a little boy in my sight?

7. Has our marriage turned out to be what you had always hoped for when we first got married?

8. Do you look forward to sexual relationship with me?

9. Do you look forward to spending time alone with me?

10. Do you find excuses to be busy with work, other people or projects to avoid spending time with me?

Reflection

1. The feeling of romantic love is not a commodity that I have or don't have. It is rather like a bank balance that floats up or down depending on intimacy.

2. Intimacy (INTO ME SEE) is very much dependent upon open and transparent heart to heart communication.

3. Transparency is dependent upon trust and covenant security.

4. Hidden things in one's life block transparency and intimacy.

5. Hidden things will ultimately be exposed through humility or humiliation:

    a. **Humility:** A wise person confessing his true behavior and character to God and those who love him.

    b. **Humiliation:** A foolish person who has hidden his shameful behavior or character being exposed publicly for all to see.

6. Self-disclosure in humility leads to credibility and trust.

7. Soulical adultery starts when communication is blocked between a married couple, and "innocent" sharing on a heart level begins with another person.

8. Shame causes us to hide things that are wrong or embarrassing to us.

9. Lack of openness and transparency with a spouse tends to promote deception and lack of transparency with God and others.

10. Face-to-face prayer and communication creates intimacy, while side-to-side relationship creates a good business partnership.

11. Daily face-to-face prayer including repentance, thanksgiving and blessing increases intimacy and tends to reduce the risk of divorce over 500 fold.

12. It is helpful to check on how you are truly impacting your spouse by periodically taking time to honestly ask and answer **The Real Questions**.

Resources

⊙ [1] Communication in Marriage Course—*Renewing the Bond of Love* (See Appendix for details.)

🎧 Identifying Shame

📖 Marriage Under Cover (Meisner)

🎧 Soulical Adultery

chapter 8
Ways of Handling
Conflict

L et's now turn our attention to handling conflict within a
marriage. Conflict is not necessarily bad, but rather can be
used to identify root issues in the lives of the couple, and if
handled properly may be used to move the couple into greater
personal and marital freedom. However, when conflict is handled improperly, it can turn into a highly destructive force that
results in great damage to the marriage relationship.

In chapter six we talked in some detail about the fact that we
are in a battle with unseen forces in the kingdom of darkness
whose purpose it is to destroy our marriage. We also talked
about the primary strategy used against most marriages working
through blindness to the relational communication messages we
inadvertently send one another. Let's now look in a little more
detail at how conflict may degenerate into an argument. We will
then look at four ineffective ways that fleas might deal with the

situation, and one effective way for a free man or woman to resolve the conflict.

Initially arguments tend to start when one partner's identity is invalidated and he is wounded through receiving a relational message of worthlessness. As we discussed before, husbands tend to convey lack of love by **invalidating** a wife's feelings and opinions and thereby her identity. Wives tend to convey disrespect by criticizing and communicating **disapproval** to a husband. Following is a chart depicting a typical example of the escalation of communication from a calm statement to an argument.

Escalation of an Argument

Husband	Wife
1. He states an opinion or consideration.	2. Miscommunication takes place and she expresses upset feelings.
3. He justifies and explains why she shouldn't be upset about this.	4. She feels **invalidated** and becomes more upset.
5. He feels her **disapproval** and blames her for falsely accusing him.	6. She feels more invalidated, becomes more upset and the argument escalates into a battle.

As this process begins, each person has a choice as to how he will proceed. We have observed four different strategies that fleas will use in attempting to avoid the emotional pain caused by the conflict. I have outlined these strategies next.

1) **Fight:** Attack (Win/lose strategy) "We have unresolved issues for which I will fight and I'm happy only if I win."

   Tactics: Intimidation, manipulation, threat, yelling, blame, criticism, anger.

2) **Flight:** Withdraw (Lose/lose strategy) "We have unresolved issues which are not worth fighting over and I'm happy if we just leave them unresolved."

   Tactics: Avoidance; closing up; withdrawal of affection, communication, and support.

3) **Fake:** Deny and Pretend (Lose/win strategy) "We don't have any unresolved issues. I'm happy as it is and everything is fine."

   Tactics: Appeasement, denial and stuffing of feelings, appearance management, peace at all costs.

> All of these strategies focus on pain avoidance for the flea.

4) **Fold:** Give up (Lose/win strategy) "We have unresolved issues that are irresolvable. I'm not happy and never will be, so what's the point in trying?"

   Tactics: Self-pity, withdrawal, depression, and suicide threats.

As I'm sure you can see, none of these strategies work to resolve the conflict or to build a healthy relationship. All of these strategies focus on pain avoidance for the flea. None of the above four is a win/win strategy to be implemented by a free person. This would require the emotional capacity to respond with new attitudes and behavior, rather than to simply react to the attitudes and behavior of the spouse. In looking at the above strategies, it is important that you primarily take note of which strategy is the most common one in which you engage. Don't focus on which one your spouse uses.

Forgiveness From the Heart

Let's now look at a different strategy that actually is a win/win strategy. The only problem with this strategy is that it cannot easily be implemented by a flea. It takes emotional maturity and a measure of freedom in order to accomplish this task.

5) **Forgive:** Convey understanding, acceptance and forgiveness. (Win/win strategy) "We have unresolved *topical* issues for which there is a solution that meets both of our desires and goals, but can only be arrived at when we have understood and resolved our *relational* issues."

Tactics:
a) Discern the relational messages received and sent.
b) Seek to understand why your partner sent you the relational message he did. Separate identity from behavior. (Remove the log from your eye so that you can deal with the speck in your partner's eye.)
c) Forgive your partner from your heart for hurting you.
d) Apologize to your partner and ask for him to forgive you for disapproving of, or invalidating, his identity.
e) Now work together to find a solution acceptable to both husband and wife for the topical issue.

I have noticed that many people battle with forgiving their spouse particularly when the wound is deep and the offence is particularly serious. Let's first talk about what forgiveness is and what it is not.

Forgiveness is not forgetting, excusing, tolerating, overlooking, condoning, justifying that there really wasn't a problem, or allowing others to regularly violate my boundaries and take advantage of me.

Forgiveness is releasing another person from accountability for their wrongdoing, sin, mistake, failure, disappointment or betrayal of me. Although forgiveness is frequently a process, it begins with a choice I make. A key understanding I have gained in forgiveness is that it is not necessary for the other person to be repentant or even understand or acknowledge his sin in order for me to forgive him. Unforgiveness is an emotional poison that will harm me, not the person who sinned against me. So it makes no sense for me to hold poison within me that is toxic to me simply because another person doesn't recognize his sin.

Forgiveness entails releasing the other person from accountability and the desire to have him "pay" for what he did. I have come to realize that Jesus Christ did not only die to pay for my sin against God and others, but also to pay for the sins of others against me. So when I, through unforgiveness, hold someone else accountable to pay for his own sin against me, I am actually refusing to receive payment made by God of the covenant blood of Jesus Christ. I am in reality standing outside the door of God's eternal tabernacle where His blood was poured out, and am refusing to step across the threshold and come in to receive the benefits He is offering me in covenant. Once I realized this, it has then been easier to let Jesus pay for others' sin rather than for me to hold another person accountable to pay for his own sin and wrongdoing.

In intellectually understanding this, I have found that it is still sometimes very difficult to truly forgive from the heart. Even when I have made a choice in my mind to forgive, sometimes my heart still won't release the hurt, anger or resentment. I'm sure you have experienced the same. In Matthew 18:35, after a lengthy parable about forgiveness, Jesus instructs us that when someone sins against us we are to **forgive him from the heart.**

I have thought much about what it might mean to forgive someone from the heart. I know that it certainly is possible to forgive someone from the mind, but not from the heart. Have you ever "tried" to forgive someone, but in reality your heart won't release him? It is just too painful and the wound is too deep. But being the mature godly person that you are, you make the choice to forgive, anyway.

"Alright Lord, I forgive him." You pray the prayer and release the person. You feel a little better, having done the "right" thing and it seems better. All is well for the next couple of days until you see that person again. Then all of the feelings of hurt and betrayal are stirred back up again, and you think,

"He got away with it scot-free. I'm the one who was damaged and nothing happened to him. It's not fair."

Then you remember, "Oh yeah. I forgot. I forgave him. Jesus paid for what he did. I forgive him again."

You may go through several cycles of this, but the hurt, resentment and anger in your heart doesn't ever really go away. You have made the choice. You have forgiven him (by faith) from your mind, but you heart has not truly forgiven.

I believe that many people have gone through the frustration of wanting to forgive from the heart, but not truly being able to do so. The frustration is that the feelings in your heart are not under your volitional control. You cannot just will feelings to come and go from your heart on a short-term basis. You cannot simply decide to have the feeling of love to come, bitterness to go, depression to go, anger to go, or joy to come in your heart. It would be nice if life worked that way, but it doesn't.

However, I have discovered that these powerful emotions are frequently indicators of other wounds deep in the heart that have never been dealt with or healed. When these deeper wounds are healed, then the feeling of forgiveness automatically is manifested in the heart without effort or willful trying. We'll talk about how to utilize conflict to identify and heal deeper emotional wounds in the next chapter.

Unforgiveness Is an Indicator of Idolatry

Many years ago, I also discovered that unforgiveness was not in and of itself a problem, but was actually only an indicator of a problem. Thus unforgiveness is like the oil light in your car. The light is not the problem; the light is only the indicator of the problem. So it would be ridiculous for someone to work at eliminating the red light on the dashboard, rather than using the red light to discover the problem the light was indicating.

In the case of unforgiveness, it is really just an indicator of idolatry. When the Lord first confronted me with the idolatry of my unforgiveness, I didn't understand. I only understood idolatry in terms of worshiping wooden or stone "gods" fashioned by human hands. However I came to understand that idolatry is more that this. Whatever you look to as a source of life is a god to you. If you grant a place of authority in your life to a person or thing to determine your identity and/or destiny, in reality you have made that person or object a god in your life. Looking to that person or object for life instead of to God then really is a form of idolatry.

> As a flea, I was still looking to that person for value and life rather than looking to God.

I began to understand that when someone deeply wounded or betrayed me, I was actually then granting that person a place of authority in my life to tell me who I am. As a flea, I was still looking to that person for value and life rather than looking to God. Inevitably, that person then would disappoint me, hurt me, betray me, or fail to give me life, and would send me a relational message that I'm worthless. Instead of relating immediately to God to receive the truth about me, I would then unwittingly exalt that person into the place of authority in my life, and grant him permission to tell me who I am. That is the idolatry. If someone stole from me, lied about me, or did something that I perceived to damage my destiny, block my goals or set me back in life, I again would grant that person a position of authority to determine my future. The most common person to whom most people grant a place of idolatry is a husband or wife.

I have sometimes heard someone proclaim regarding a father, spouse or someone else, "You don't understand! He ruined my life."

If I make such a proclamation, I am actually authorizing the one who sinned against me to determine my future and my destiny. In my sight, that person is proclaimed to be even more powerful than God, Himself, in that he has been granted permission to determine my future and "ruin my life." Such a statement indicates to whom I am looking to determine identity and/or destiny. The one who has wounded has then been allowed to become a god and the wounded person has entered into idolatry. Unforgiveness then, is the natural protective mechanism of the heart to keep the person who sinned against me from hurting me again.

As long as I am in idolatry, and keep the one who sinned against me in that place of being a god to me, determining my identity or controlling my destiny, then try as I might, my heart will not forgive him. Thus, unforgiveness becomes an indicator to me that I am in idolatry towards another person and probably don't realize it. The ultimate problem is that I am not truly relating to God and trusting Him on a heart level to tell me who I am, and to be in charge of my future and my destiny. This can be remedied by:

1) Renouncing the idolatry.

2) Removing the one who sinned against me from that place of authority in my life.

3) Restoring God alone back to that rightful place of authority.

4) Forgiving from the heart, which now becomes possible, when I am no longer looking to the offender as my source of identity or destiny.

If you have struggled with forgiving your spouse, and are now recognizing that you have granted him that place in your life that only God Almighty should occupy, you may want to pray from your heart a prayer similar to the following.

"Father God, I recognize today that I have granted my wife (husband) a place in my heart that only You should occupy. I have been looking to her (him) as a source of life. I have let her (him) answer my identity and destiny questions. Lord God, today I recognize that this is idolatry, and that only You should occupy that position in my heart.

So today, I renounce my idolatry. Father, forgive me for looking to someone else to be my god and bring me life. I remove _____(name of your spouse) from that position of being god to me and grant You alone, Almighty God, that place of authority in my heart. I revoke the authority I gave to _____ (name of your spouse) to tell me who I am or to determine my future. I place myself, and my future in Your hands alone, and I declare that You are God and my Source of life. Right now, Lord I need to hear from You. Who do You say I am? What do You say about me and about my future? (Now just wait for a few seconds and listen.)

I recognize that Jesus Christ died and shed His blood in covenant to forgive _____(name of your spouse) for her (his) sins and wrongdoing against me. Today I receive the blood of Your covenant in payment for the wrongs done to me by _____(name of your spouse). I declare that Your blood is enough, and because You have paid I now forgive _____ (name of your spouse) for all her (his) mistakes, shortcomings, sins, betrayals, and wrongdoing against me. I now pray that You also heal and bless _____ (name of your spouse). Amen."

Reflection

1. Four unhealthy ways to respond to conflict.
   a. **Fight:** Attack. (Win/lose strategy.)
   b. **Flight:** Withdraw. (Lose/lose strategy.)
   c. **Fake:** Deny and Pretend. (Lose/win strategy.)
   d. **Fold:** Give up. (Lose/win strategy.)
2. One healthy way to respond to conflict.

      a. **Forgive:** Convey understanding, acceptance and forgiveness. (Win/win strategy.)

3. **Forgiveness is** releasing another person from accountability for their wrongdoing, sin, mistake, failure, disappointment or betrayal of me.

4. Forgiveness from the heart is not just a matter of a decision of the will.

5. Unforgiveness is actually an indicator of idolatry, and the empowerment of another person into the place in my heart that only God should occupy.

6. True forgiveness from the heart comes automatically when the love of God removes the fear caused by the identity ("I have no value") and welfare ("My needs and goals won't be met") lies deep in my heart.

Resources

⊙ 1 Communication in Marriage Course—*Renewing the Bond of Love* (See Appendix for details.)

🎧   Why Does My Husband Remind Me of My Dad

chapter 9

Using Conflict to
Identify Root Issues

Most married couples view conflict as a very negative occurrence. As we have seen in previous chapters, if it is not handled properly, conflict can result in great damage and destruction to a marital relationship. However, if recognized and properly utilized, conflict can be used to help identify deep emotional lies and roots of destructive behavior.

Through the years, Jan and I have encountered many couples who have been very frustrated by their own inability to change destructive emotional response patterns and behavior in their own lives. Both the husband and wife have come to the place of understanding that they need to deal with their own personal dysfunction, not try to change the attitudes and behavior of their spouse. However, even with this goal, many have still experienced a deep frustration in their own inability to change.

Behavior Modification vs. True Freedom

I believe that this frustration is rooted in a widespread misconception that by the power of my own will, I really can change and control my own emotions and behavior. This is simply not the truth. Anyone who has ever gone on a "diet" can attest to this. Many Christians believe this, but simply couch their misbelief in biblical vernacular. In reality, the belief that I really do have the power to change myself is nothing more than humanistic behavior modification.

When a person encounters a destructive attitude or behavior such as anger, resentment, fear, depression, lust, pride or worthlessness, the first thing he usually tries is to simply "stop it." He believes that somehow by greater self-effort, more intense determination, and will power this will change. Many times people then engage in several of the following tactics: try harder, get some counseling, go to church more frequently, pray more, memorize more scripture, fast, cast out demons, receive medication. Some strong willed people are able to control some external symptoms, but the inner root is still there. In many cases, much of what I have heard Christians call "walking in victory" is actually just symptom management. The root inner compulsion is still working, but the person is able to "control" the external manifestation most of the time.

I believe that the reason these activities usually don't help is because they are not really getting at the root of these external problems. In other words, people are attempting to get the red oil light in their car to quit flashing at them. A hammer, bashing out the red light, is effective to eliminate the light. However, since the light was only the indicator of the underlying problem, the problem still remains, and the person is actually now worse off, as he now has no light to let him know there is a problem.

Heart Truth vs. Mind Truth

What if there really are roots to these externals and when the roots are exposed and removed, the external feeling and behavior ceases to manifest simply because the compelling force behind it has been removed? I have found that this actually is true. Telling someone to stop drinking, viewing pornography, yelling at the children, being angry, or hating, is not helpful in terminating this behavior because these are only external indicators of deep inner brokenness and heart lies. However, what if we could utilize the conflict frequently stirred up in marriage like an oil light in a car to identify these root heart lies within both husband and wife and replace them with truth? Jesus talked about exactly this process in John 8:32.

"And you shall know the truth, and the truth shall set you free" (John 8:32).

We often see this scripture verse written on the entrance to libraries and such places. However, the revelation that changed my life is that the "truth" about which Jesus was speaking here is not cognitive, intellectual truth. It is deep-rooted experiential, emotional heart truth. Truth received and rooted in the heart is very different than truth rooted only in the mind.

> What if we could utilize the conflict frequently stirred up in marriage like an oil light in a car to identify these root heart lies within both husband and wife and replace them with truth?

For example, consider the phrase, "I know how to fly." Which is more important: experiential heart truth or cognitive mind truth? Two people could both honestly make the above statement. One has just passed the Private Pilot written exam with a 100% score, but has never piloted an airplane. The other person got a 72% score on his Private Pilot written exam ten years ago and has 5000 hours of pilot experience. Which person really "knows" how to fly? With which one would you rather take a flight in an airplane?

Along the same lines, suppose you have a child who wakes up shortly after going to bed screaming that there are monsters under his bed. You go into your son's bedroom, turn on the light and help him look under his bed. You then show him every nook and cranny under the bed and explain to him that there are no monsters under his bed. You even secure his agreement that you both have just thoroughly searched under the bed in the light, and there are no monsters there. You ask if he believes that there are no monsters in his room and under his bed, and he replies affirmatively. You then tuck him back in bed, turn out the light and leave, only to have him screaming that the monsters are back under his bed a few minutes later. Does the cognitive truth that the monsters don't exist and that they are not under his bed help your son? NO! Why? Because the lie is not cognitive, but rather is emotional, and is in his heart.

So, the truth that sets people free is not cognitive, intellectual mind truth, but rather is deep-rooted, experiential, emotional heart truth. Let's now think about the converse of this principle. If deep-rooted experiential heart truth from God will set me free, then could it be that deep-rooted, experiential heart lies from the enemy will put me in bondage and keep me there? Certainly! Furthermore, these heart lies are at the root of most marital conflict. If this is understood, then conflict in my marriage can be used to uncover and remove the compelling forces that drive destructive attitudes and behavior in my life. Let me further explain what I mean.

Again, I think that all of human experience can only be understood within the context of the spiritual battle described in Ephesians 6:10-20. From the day that each of us are conceived, we are caught up in a battle between God and the devil over who gets to impart on a heart level inner emotional images of our identity and destiny. Satan is seeking to impart potent experiential lies into our hearts regarding God, self, others, and life.

God, on the other hand, is seeking to impart truth into our hearts in these same areas. I have found that Satan's experiential lies are primarily imparted through traumatic or wounding experiences with people, especially family members, in childhood.

All of us were emotionally wounded as children in various ways, even by well-meaning parents. Consequently, all of us carry varying degrees of unresolved emotional wounds, insecurities, fear, shame and lies into our adult lives. As we walk through our adult life, these hidden emotional fears and lies are "triggered" by present circumstances and people. When one of these insecurities or lies is triggered, we may experience a very potent emotional response to the present person or circumstance. Because we are tapping into not only the emotion of the moment, but also into the stored emotion from past wounding experiences, the emotion manifested may be much stronger than the present circumstance would warrant.

This is why you may experience in yourself or your spouse a reaction to a present circumstance that seems to be totally unwarranted. For example: "All I said was, 'Blah, blah, blah,' and he is responding as if I had killed someone." Why is this? It is because you have just tapped into a deep-rooted heart lie charged with lots of emotion from past wounding. The first step toward resolving this is, as we discussed earlier, to terminate discussion on the topical level and deal with the relational messages sent.

However, if you understand the overall battle, you have an even greater opportunity to identify and eliminate the deep-rooted heart lie from which this potent emotional reaction is emanating. There is an opportunity to replace that lie with the truth on a heart level and bring true freedom to that area of your life. If you truly understand this, whenever your spouse triggers in you powerful emotions emanating from deep rooted heart lies, you ought to thank him rather than be angry. You have a unique opportunity to win a great personal victory in your life, and enter into a whole new realm of personal freedom.

Viruses In the Heart (Hard) Drive

Let me share with you an analogy that has helped me understand this process of utilizing conflict to identify and remove heart lies. This analogy requires some knowledge of computer technology, which many people have these days. God has created all of us as human beings with both a mind and a heart. I believe that the mind and heart could be described as two separate hard drives of the human computer with a firewall in between them. This means that by and large, data that is stored in the heart/emotional drive is not normally accessible to the mind/intellectual drive. Emotionally painful and wounding experiences seem to be stored primarily in the heart drive. If they are particularly painful, they seem to be stored in a "vault" section of the heart drive that is sealed and not easily or normally accessible. Many times, embedded in the file containing the record of these experiences are very potent, compulsive viruses.

> You have a unique opportunity to win a great personal victory in your life, and enter into a whole new realm of personal freedom.

How were these viruses embedded in such files? The Bible tells us that there is a thief (hacker) whose purpose is to steal, kill, and destroy (John 10:10). The legal term for burglary, the activity of thieves, is "breaking and entering." So, beginning when we are small children, the thief (hacker) seeks to use people and circumstances to break and enter our hearts, and deposit viruses. A virus is really a hidden program designed to disrupt the normal operation of the computer at inopportune times. The type of viruses we are speaking about are lies containing fear and other potent associated emotions, cloaked in darkness, and deposited in files deep within the heart drive. These viruses are then programmed to manifest certain external system malfunctions when stimulated by specific external stimuli. The file in which a virus is embedded normally contains the record of the original experience through which the thief was able to implant the original virus (lie).

So in this analogy we have three components:

- **Current system malfunction**: Potent current manifesting emotion, behavior or addiction.

- **Host File in which the virus is embedded**: Memory of the original wounding experience.

- **Virus**: The original emotional lie.

One of the reasons that this strategy of the enemy works so well is that the virus is not accessible, and many times not even known by the intellectual mind drive. Sometimes a file containing a record of the original wounding experience is cognitively available in the mind drive, but the emotional lie (virus) is not accessible or even detected. As a matter of fact, a virus detection program will not be able to access the vault in the heart drive, and will report to you that the entire computer is clean and there are no viruses detected. This is why we have found that it is not possible to "talk" people out of their emotional lies. You can try all you want to convince that child that there are no monsters under his bed, but the lie (virus) which is emotional, not intellectual, is not removed because it is embedded in a file in the heart drive, not the mind drive.

Once I understood this, it explained to me why many current "sin management" programs in the church have not produced the desired results. As long as the virus remains intact in the heart, the external addiction, compulsion, or problem will not go away, no matter how long you pray or fast, or how sincerely you repent and cry before God, asking Him to change you.

In the computer analogy, if there is a virus affecting your operating system, resulting in malfunctions in a peripheral program, it won't help you to get a "patch" for the peripheral program. If Windows is broken, never mind an MS Word or Excel patch. You need to deal with the virus affecting Windows, which affects all of your peripheral programs. (I apologize to Mac users. I'm sure you still get the analogy, anyway.)

So trying to stop pride, lust, anger, lying, or drinking is like applying a patch to these external applications while leaving the virus in place in the heart operating system. Instead, you need to identify, quarantine, eliminate the virus, and then replace it with files and programs containing truth.

Let me give you a couple of practical examples.

External experience: Sandy is cold, unresponsive, and often becomes emotionally upset during sexual intimacy with her husband. She experiences feelings of sorrow, uncleanness, guilt, shame, and wanting to flee at these times. She doesn't want to hurt her husband, so initially she lies to him, pretending that the experience is pleasurable for her. However, she cannot maintain this front for long, and soon the truth comes out. Sometimes when her husband approaches her, all Sandy can do is lie there and weep. When her husband asks her what is wrong, she can't even find words to explain to him the deep feeling of sorrow and grief, nor the reason for it. She tries to assure him that it has nothing to do with him, but this is unintelligible to him.

Try as she might, Sandy cannot make these feelings during sexual intimacy go away. In her mind drive (intellectually) she knows the truth, that sexual intimacy in marriage is right, pure, blessed by God, and the celebration of a covenant. She loves her husband and wants to be free to experience what God intended for her in married sexual intimacy. However, no matter how hard she tries to embrace this intellectual truth, her experience of sexual intimacy with her husband is always overshadowed by these powerful feelings in her heart.

Sandy's response to her husband is now causing him to feel that there must be something wrong with him as a man, to be so undesirable and displeasing to his wife. This is now affecting his self-esteem as a man, and creating significant tension and conflict within their marriage.

Current malfunction: Feelings of sorrow, uncleanness, guilt, shame, and wanting to run away accompanying any mention of, or initiation of sexual relationship with her husband.

Host file: Sexual violation by an uncle at age five.

Virus: Emotional lies: "It was my fault I was violated because I was wearing a swimming suit that attracted my uncle. Sexual relationship is dirty and defiling. I'm spoiled now. I will never be clean. I am powerless and unprotected, and men will hurt me whenever I am vulnerable."

Hopefully you can see that no amount of counseling, in an attempt to convince Sandy that sexual relationship within marriage is pure and right, will change the feelings in her heart. The virus in the heart must be accessed and replaced with the emotional truth that will set her free. This can only happen when the heart drive is open, and the Holy Spirit removes the lie and imparts His truth. I will explain in the next section how you can begin to learn how to facilitate this process for each other as a married couple. Here is another example.

External experience: John is a workaholic. He owns his own business and is never home or available physically or emotionally for his wife or children. John is also harsh and critical of his wife and children. He generates a significant income and is quite prosperous, but no matter how much he makes, it seems like it is never enough. John's wife complains to him and asks him to be more available to her and the children. This angers him, and he tells her he is working to provide for her and the kids.

Current malfunction: Feelings of anger, deep sense of failure, never being a success, and never achieving enough, no matter how hard he works.

Host file: When he was six years old, John was not doing well in school. One day his father, a wealthy businessman, took him for a ride in his new luxury automobile and proclaimed, "Enjoy the ride, son, because you will never have a car like this. You're stupid and will never amount to anything."

Virus: Emotional lies—"I'm stupid. I'll never make any money. I'll never amount to anything. No matter how hard I work, I will never succeed and win my father's approval. The only way to ever be accepted is to make more money and work harder."

Because of the deep-rooted (virus) heart lie, working hard was a compulsion for John. Even though it makes no logical sense, John's virus even compelled him to speak to his six-year old son, who was also doing poorly in 1st grade, the exact same words that his father had spoken to him. Now John had effectively been used by the enemy to implant the same virus into the heart of another generation in his family. Obviously, it would do no good to try to counsel him and convince him to spend more time with his wife and children and not to wound his children in the same way he had been wounded. Until the lie was removed and replaced with the truth, John was not able to change his external pattern of workaholism, and harsh criticism, even though he intellectually knew it was destroying his marriage and family.

Victory vs. Abstinence

So, in both of these examples with Sandy and John, as long as the lies remain imbedded emotionally in the heart, the feelings and external behavior will remain unchanged. Some very strong-willed people are able to curb and change some of the external behavior through sheer determination, will power and elaborate "current malfunction patches." Then, when there is no regular external manifestation, the person declares victory.

However, the battle remains the same inside and there is a daily internal battle to maintain this "victory." In reality, this person is not experiencing authentic personal victory, but rather just external abstinence. Militarily, victory is not declared when you have merely set up a perimeter and contained all enemy combatants, but they still shoot at you daily and try to penetrate the perimeter. Victory is declared when all enemy combatants are either dead or disarmed and incarcerated. The battle has totally ceased and no one is shooting at you. This is victory.

Obviously, God's goal is not for you to just manage the current malfunction, but rather to identify the virus and remove it. When this happens, the host file record of the experience remains in the heart, but it is no longer emotionally charged. Consequently, there is simply no longer a battle, and no more experience of current malfunction. **This is true victory and remains maintenance-free.** I have found that you can't really facilitate this process for yourself. It is something that the Holy Spirit has to do in your heart for you.

> The battle has totally ceased and no one is shooting at you. This is victory.

In order to experience and learn this process by which the Holy Spirit can remove heart viruses and replace them with truth, I would highly suggest that you consider attending an *Ancient Paths Seminar*,[1] which is designed to facilitate exactly this process in your life. Once you have had this experience for yourself in a seminar environment, it will be much easier to learn how to facilitate the ministry process regularly for each other within the context of your own marriage.

---

[1] To find and *Ancient Paths Seminar* near you go to the FFI website at: www.familyfoundations.com

Identifying and Removing Viruses

If you understand that underneath the powerful emotions frequently stirred up by marital conflict there are viruses, you can then utilize these unique times when the heart drive is wide open to follow the external manifest feeling right back to the host file and virus in the heart. It is not normally possible to do this when the emotion is not stirred and presently manifesting. Most of the time, we find that the virus (deep-rooted emotional lie) is not accessible because the mind drive is dominant.

However, the virus usually becomes accessible when it is triggered by a present person or circumstance (namely your spouse). So the triggering of the virus and the potent emotional feelings that accompany it provide a special window in time to identify it, and deal with it. Conflict, then provides a unique opportunity for healing and freedom. In most cases your spouse is uniquely designed by God to trigger your specific viruses better than anyone else. This is why I said earlier, that when a spouse triggers one of your viruses, you ought to thank him rather than curse him.

The process for healing that Jan and I have effectively used is as follows. When conflict arises and one or both of us have emotional viruses triggered, we first must make a decision to exercise the available opportunity for healing. This may be difficult, as it requires making a choice, despite the emotion, to initiate the virus-removal process (software) rather than to pursue the conflict. If we are both triggered, we must then decide which one of us we will pray for. Once we have made that selection, we can then begin to pray.

The goal of our prayer is to invite God the Father by His Holy Spirit to identify the host file, and the lie it contains. We will then ask Him to speak truth into the heart and replace the lie with the truth, which we know will set us free. We want to invite the Lord then to displace three things with their opposites.

- **Lies with Truth** (John 8:32 *"You will know the truth and the truth will set you free."*)

- **Fear with Love** (John 4:18 *"Perfect love casts out fear."*)

- **Darkness with Light** (I John 1:5-7 *God is light and in Him is no darkness at all."*)

Let me now give you the practical steps of how to pray for your spouse.

Begin by accessing the file containing the virus in the person being prayed for, and then identify the virus itself. You can do this by asking your spouse what is the overwhelming feeling that he is experiencing right at that moment. You then want to ask the Lord to bring to the person's remembrance the original, root experience in which the specified strong emotion first occurred. (Wait quietly. In most cases, this will happen within a very short period of time.)

You can then isolate the virus by getting the person to speak out the lie that was deposited in that experience. Ask him to speak out what the feeling was when that experience happened.

You may then ask the Lord to impart truth, love and light into the memory of that experience. We usually pray something such as "Father God, what is the truth? What did you want to say to ____(spouse's name) at that time?"

We have discovered that all viruses are retained by anchors of fear and lies. When these anchors are removed by love and truth, the virus is automatically purged and deleted from that file. The file remains, but is totally benign. One can remember the experience, but there is no more pain or strong emotion in the memory whatsoever.

> This is authentic victory which is permanent and maintenance free.

Future words or events that used to trigger this lie and its emotional response no longer have any affect. They are devoid of ability to trigger, as there is no longer a virus there to trigger. This is authentic victory, which is permanent and maintenance free. It doesn't take discipline or will power to retain the experience of victory.

Any battle left is an indication that the virus still remains in the file and is stimulating a viral reaction to current data. In this case, there is still a need for more prayer.

Naked and Ashamed

I would now like to share with you one personal experience I had in which Jan and I utilized a potential conflict for healing and freedom. We had traveled out of town to minister at a conference and a Sunday morning church service. The pastor of the church had graciously invited us to stay with him, his wife and his mother in his home. We had accepted his invitation and were enjoying getting to know him and his family.

On Sunday morning, Jan and I got up and were getting ready for the church service. The bathroom we were to use was across the hall from the bedroom in which we were sleeping. I went across to the bathroom to take a shower, while Jan remained in the bedroom to curl her hair. When I finished my shower, I realized that I had neglected to take a shirt or bathrobe with me into the bathroom and that I would have to return across the hall to our bedroom without a shirt. Now I have been to the beach before without a shirt, but I didn't know this pastor well, and I felt that it would be a bit rude to be walking around his house in front of his wife and mother with no shirt on.

I peaked out the bathroom door and noticed that he, his wife and mother were seated at the breakfast table in the kitchen at far end of the hallway. I thought that I could quickly dash across the hallway and into our bedroom while they were busy talking with each other and that way not be noticed. So, at the opportune moment, I quickly slipped across the hallway and pushed the bedroom door to open it. However, unbeknownst to me, Jan had opened the closet door just inside the room, which blocked the bedroom door from opening more than a couple of inches.

As I attempted to open the door, after just a couple of inches it slammed with a loud bang against the closet door. At this point, the pastor and his family all turned to see what was going on. There I was, half naked, standing in the hallway waving, attempting to smile and say, "Good Morning."

I was looking into our room and snarling at Jan, "Jan open this door! Right now!" Jan was sitting on the other side of the bed curling her hair and not moving fast enough for me. After what seemed to me to be an eternity, I retreated back into the bathroom.

By this time I was furious. "Why did she just leave the closet door open? Surely she knew I was coming back into the bedroom. It is her fault that I was embarrassed in front of the pastor, his wife and even his mother." I was filled with rage toward my wife and as soon as the bedroom door was opened, I wanted to go in and let her know what she had done to me. However, as I was waiting in the bathroom for Jan to get the closet door closed so I could come in, the thought came to me that I was experiencing some very potent anger resulting from a relatively insignificant event. I knew that I had a choice to make as to whether I would spew my rage all over my wife, just bury it and try to make the anger go away, or use it to find what I now suspected might be a virus.

As I came back into the room, it was difficult for me not to spew my anger all over Jan. But I said to her, "Would you please pray for me? I am full of anger and I'm pretty sure that it must be coming from some past wounding experience." She agreed to help me pray.

We just prayed a very simple prayer, "Father God, I feel embarrassed, ashamed, angry, hateful and I want revenge. Please show me where all of these feelings first started in my life?" We then waited, and as is typical, within about 10 or 15 seconds I was remembering an experience.

I was about 7 or 8 years old in second grade at school. Our class had gone together to use the lavatory facilities. We were then walking in a single file line back to our classroom. For some reason, one of the children at the front of the line decided to begin to shuffle and slide his feet along as he walked. This caught on, and soon the entire class was doing the same. I was somewhere in the middle of the line and was shuffling and sliding my feet along the same as everyone else.

All of a sudden, the teacher grabbed me by the arm, jerked me out of the line and began to yell at me. She told me she was taking me to the principal's office and he would talk with me. As she dragged me down the hall toward the principal's office, I still had no idea what I had done wrong. I was just doing the same thing that all of the other boys and girls in my class were doing, shuffling our feet. When I arrived at the principal's office, I finally discovered what crime I had committed. Unbeknownst to me, I had forgotten to zip up the fly of my pants after using the restroom facilities. Consequently, while I was shuffling my feet the same as all of the other children, because my fly was open the teacher thought that this was purposeful and I was doing something lewd or sexually explicit. Of course at that age, I was not even awake yet to sexual things, and I had no idea that my fly was unzipped.

The principal then lectured me, and I was made to feel that there was really something very evil and wrong with me. I felt very embarrassed, unjustly accused, shamed, unfairly picked out, and given no opportunity for explanation or response. As a result, I hated that teacher, wanted to somehow punish her and let her know what it felt like to be singled out and embarrassed for no reason. I also wanted to somehow protect myself so that such embarrassment would never happen to me again.

Back in our bedroom as I was reliving this experience and all of these feelings, Jan then prayed another very simple prayer, "Lord, You were there that day. You saw what happened to Craig. Would you please speak to him the truth about who he is and what You wanted him to know that day."

Immediately I began to hear the voice of the Father. He said, "Son, I love you. I never wanted that to happen to you that day. Your teacher simply made a mistake. She made you feel that there was something wrong with you and you let her identity message take root in your heart. You didn't come to Me and ask Me for the truth. Son, there's nothing wrong with you. You don't have to protect yourself. Your teacher can't pay for the shame and embarrassment she wrongfully caused you. But I did pay for that with the blood of Jesus Christ. Would you forgive her and let My blood be enough to pay for her wrongdoing, and damage of you?"

I then responded, "Yes Lord. Your blood is enough. I forgive the teacher. Please forgive me for not running to You, but instead receiving her assessment of me and vowing to isolate and protect myself from then on."

I then heard the Lord say, "You don't have to worry about being embarrassed before others any more. You are loved and valuable and I will always be with you and protect you. You can allow yourself to be vulnerable and still be safe."

As I was interacting with the Lord, I was not only hearing His words, but I was also feeling the powerful emotion of His love and protection for me. I began to weep as His love was entering into that place in my heart that was fearful, insecure, feeling that I would be judged and embarrassed due to no fault of my own. As His love filled that place, it experientially drove out all of that fear and insecurity. Along with it went the anger, hatred, resentment, and embarrassment.

After the Lord had finished speaking to me, I was amazed to find that all of the anger that had been so strong toward Jan just a minute ago was gone. As we talked about what had just taken place, there was no longer any offence or emotion in it at all for me. I didn't have to try to make it go. It just wasn't there. I didn't have to try to forgive her. There was no offence there to forgive. It had already happened in my heart. Now it just seemed like a funny incident.

I also then returned to the memory of what had happened with the teacher in school. I could still remember all of the details, but that memory was also devoid of any emotion. I was no longer hateful or angry toward the teacher or principal. I saw what had happened, but there was no painful emotion in it any longer for me. Because of this, I knew that I had experientially received the truth in my heart and the truth had set me free (John 8:32).

I was so free that I actually shared the experience of what the Lord had just done in me with the church congregation that morning. The pastor, his wife and mother laughed about it, as there was no more shame or embarrassment in the experience for me. I then thanked Jan for leaving the closet door open so that I couldn't get back into the bedroom. By doing so she had triggered a virus of which I was totally unaware, so that we were able to find it, and I could get free of it. So, rather than damaging our marriage relationship, this incident turned out to benefit us and bring a greater trust and intimacy into our marriage.

I realized that without this experience, I would never have known why, nor been free of the anger and resentment I had frequently felt when someone embarrassed me in front of others. So Jan and I have grown to use instances of potential conflict to identify viruses that may still be working in us from past wounding experiences to receive the truth from the Lord and get free. If you have this understanding, then conflict with your spouse becomes your friend rather than your enemy. We have found, however, that because we were regularly using conflict between us to our advantage in this way, we now very rarely have the opportunity to experience such conflict any more. It just doesn't seem to happen much. I suspect that from a spiritual warfare perspective, when the devil finds a scheme that no longer works effectively, he probably avoids its use. So Jan and I now have to look for other opportunities to identify and deal with viruses that yet remain in us.

Reflection

1. Self-effort, will power, and determination to change will only yield external behavior modification, but never true freedom.

2. External problems are only the indicator (oil light) of a much deeper root "virus" within the heart.

3. The truth that actually sets one free is experiential heart truth, not cognitive mind truth.

4. Three key components usually causing marital conflict:

   a. Current system malfunction: Potent current emotion, behavior or addiction.

   b. Host File in which the virus is embedded: Memory of the original wounding experience.

   c. Virus: The original emotional lie.

5. True personal victory is accompanied by the total absence of battle. Abstinence, sometimes mistaken for victory, may be produced by controlling an external behavior, while the same internal battle as before continues to rage.

6. True heart freedom and personal victory is complete and maintenance-free.

7. A virus embedded in a file in the heart drive is not normally accessible to the mind drive.

8. When conflict has "triggered" a virus in the heart drive, there is a unique opportunity to work together with your spouse to identify and remove that virus right at that moment.

9. Conflict with your spouse that triggers emotion in you is your unique opportunity to identify and replace a hidden virus with truth, and become in actuality free in that area.

Resources

1   *An Ancient Paths Seminar*: Blessing Generations (or The Ancient Paths Seminar). See Appendix for details and www.familyfoundations.com for schedule of upcoming events.

📖   The Ancient Paths

🎧   Living Free of Anger and Frustration

🎧   The Truth About Deception; Part 3: Dynamics of Deception

chapter 10
Bridging the
Grand Canyon

I n the second chapter of this book I spoke about four different stages of marriage. We have found that it is very difficult for couples that are in the drowning or flea stages to resolve conflict on their own. If you are in Stages 1 or 2, as I mentioned earlier, I highly suggest that you work through these chapters with a counselor or mentor couple. Although both husband and wife can learn the necessary principles to utilize conflict for benefit, many times couples in Stages 1 or 2 simply don't have the emotional capacity to be able to implement what they know.

This is compounded by the fact that perceived need is so great in their lives, both husband and wife have difficulty focusing on anything other than how they have been hurt and offended, and betrayed by their marriage partner. One of the primary indicators of fleadom still significantly working in your life is that your primary thought in each chapter thus far has been that your spouse really needs to read this.

We have worked with some couples who have already done tremendous damage to their relationship before we got to know them. The image I have had sometimes is that they have already wounded each other to such a large extent that the distance between them is like the Grand Canyon. He is standing on one side, and she is standing on the other. Each is saying, "If he would just abandon his selfish, prideful, fearful, manipulative (or whatever other areas of sin might be present) position and come across to this side, the marriage could be healed and all would be fine." Of course this doesn't happen and both remain on either side of the Grand Canyon.

In this situation, I have found a few simple initial steps that a couple can take to stop widening the gap between them, and to begin the process of healing and restoration. One couple we worked with was in this situation and seemingly continuing to widen the gap between them. At one point, after talking and praying with both of them numerous times, Jan and I felt led to send them a letter containing three of these principles we felt would be useful. I have copied excerpts of this letter below. If you find yourself standing on either side of the Grand Canyon, the principles we shared with Dan and Carol (not their real names) may also be of some help to you.

Confess Your Own Sins

Dear Dan and Carol,

Jan and I have been diligently praying for you both and for your marriage over the last several months. We feel that it is time that we share with you both together some things we see that may potentially be very offensive to you or may help you, depending on your response to them.

Firstly, you are each very aware of the others' wrongdoing, and in your relationship together, you both have become very focused on the sins, errors and blind spots of your spouse. This has created tremendous negative destructive momentum in the spirit realm and in the natural. You are both killing the spirit of your marriage through your accusation and focus upon the sin of each other.

Dan, most of the e-mails we get from you ask us to pray for Carol and to please talk to Carol regarding the ways that she is hurting you and has sinned against you. Carol, most of the e-mails we receive from you ask us to pray for Dan and to please talk to Dan regarding his sins, deception and the way he has hurt you. We would agree with you both in much of the correct identification of sin and deception working within your spouse. However, focusing on the wrongdoing of your spouse will not change your spouse. You can only take responsibility for letting God change you. A focus on freedom from your own sin and deception we believe would bring about change in the relationship much more rapidly. We haven't yet received many e-mails from either of you requesting prayer for exposure and freedom from your own sin and emotionally immature responses to each other.

> Focusing on the wrongdoing of your spouse will not change your spouse.

There is a principle outlined in James 5:16 that tells us *"Confess your trespasses (sins, faults) to one another, and pray for one another that you may be healed."* It seems that you both have transposed this principle into **"Confess your marriage partner's sins** to each other and to your 'prayer partners' that you might be healed." So far as we can see, no healing has yet come from this. May we suggest that for the time being your e-mail, phone, or personal communication with each other be **limited to confessing your own sins to each other** rather than desperately trying to get the other one to change.

Secondly, each of you seems to respond as a ping pong ball whenever your spouse serves you any particular behavior or communication. You both usually punish each other when the other does not agree with you or refuses to bow to your demands.... Dan, Carol, you each have a choice to respond at each point in time to your spouse by either initiating new behavior and communication in the Spirit or by responding as an emotional ping pong ball in the flesh. Once you start a ping pong game, the ball just goes back and forth and back and forth and the childish response in the flesh intensifies in its destruction with each volley of the ball.

When will this ping pong game end? …The ping pong game will only stop when either one of you (not even both, just one) stops focusing on the wrongdoing of the other and begins to initiate new behavior in the Spirit, rather than just responding in the flesh to protect self. Jesus explained the initiation of new behavior in the Spirit as opposed to reaction in the flesh when He said, *"But I tell you not to resist an evil person. But whoever slaps you on your right cheek, turn the other to him also."* Matthew 5:39 (also see Romans 12:17-21). What does this truly mean in your personal situation?

It further seems to us that each of you is intensely interested in protecting and fulfilling self. In so doing, you are not trusting God. Dan, you are not trusting God with Carol…. Almost everything you do and say has an underlying agenda to get her to do what you want her to do, not to purely bless her. Carol, you are not trusting God by protecting yourself…. When you are trusting in your own protective measures, we believe that you are binding the hand of God from moving on your behalf. Again the biblical principle is that when you seek to save your own life, you lose the very thing you are seeking to save. *"Whoever desires to save his life will lose it, but whoever loses his life for my sake and the gospel's will save it"* (Mark 8:35).

Sarah is a good biblical example. Abraham refused to protect Sarah, but rather lied the second time and allowed the Canaanite king to take Sarah into his harem. Rather than taking matters into her own hands to protect herself, Sarah trusted God for the outcome. Sarah did not seek to save her own life. God gave the king a dream and told him that he would be killed for taking another man's wife and that she was not Abraham's sister, but rather his wife. God spared Sarah even when Abraham did not do what was right (Genesis 20:1-7). In this situation, we believe that both Abraham and Sarah were spared by Sarah's trust in God. Had she tried to save herself, both Sarah and Abraham probably would have perished.

We realize that it is very difficult not to protect yourself when you sense emotional death coming at you through your spouse. However, we have learned that it is possible, rather than to protect self and react in the flesh, to allow the death to simply pass through into the death of Christ and allow resurrection life to flow back out of Him through us to the one sending the death to us (2 Corinthians 4:7-12; Philippians 3:10). If we don't learn how to do this, then we will simply put up our own wall of protection in the flesh and try to keep the death out. This results in trusting self instead of trusting God. This is like two fleas each attempting to obtain life from the other and keep out death from each other. Or maybe the appropriate analogy is like two scorpions, who inadvertently, automatically react by stinging the other when threatened, disappointed, or the other does not provide the life the first one was looking for. Then one builds a thick wall to keep the other out so as not to be stung any further.

The opposite of the flea or scorpion analogy would be two rechargeable batteries each drawing life from the re-charger (the Lord) and then passing the life through to the other. This entails learning to let the poison of the sting pass through to Jesus and put to death the active death coming at you. You can then pass through the resurrection life of Jesus back to the one who has just stung you. Death is always swallowed up by life.

The best picture in real life we can think of is David Wilkerson's response to Nicky Cruz as recounted in the book *The Cross and the Switchblade*[1]. My paraphrase of the account is as follows: Every day David would tell Nicky that Jesus loved him. Every day Nicky would curse David. Finally one day Nicky was fed up and pinned David to the wall with a switchblade to his throat and said,

"You skinny preacher, if you tell me Jesus loves me one more time, I'm going to cut you into a thousand ribbons." (That's quite a lot of emotional death coming at you.)

David did not play ping pong with Nicky by pulling out a bigger knife like "Crocodile Dundee", or by running, or defending himself. He simply passed the death from Nicky into the death of Jesus and initiated new behavior in the Spirit in resurrection life by leaving himself vulnerable and exposed and said,

"Nicky, you can cut me into a thousand ribbons if you want, but every ribbon will still cry out, 'Jesus loves you.'"

David didn't defend his own life. Rather, he trusted the Lord with his life even when threatened with physical death. Dan, it seems to us that you are like a scorpion looking to Carol to bring you life, and when she does not meet your expectations or stings you, you inadvertently (and sometimes on purpose) sting her. Carol, it seems to us that you are like a scorpion too, looking to Dan to bring you life, and

---

[1] Wilkerson, David, The Cross and the Switchblade, (1962)
www.davidwilkerson.org

when he lures you to be with him again, he stings you, so you retreat and build a thick wall so that he cannot harm you again. In so doing, neither of you are able to be rechargeable batteries passing the poison and death from the other through to Jesus and returning resurrection life from the Lord back to your spouse who stung you. Instead you each rely on your own defensive survival kit, trusting in self to deal with the other. Please seek God about how each of you could become David Wilkerson in the face of Nicky Cruz (rechargeable batteries instead of fleas or scorpions) in relationship to your marriage partner.

Having said these things, please implement these three principles.

1. Confess your own sins, not those of your marriage partner.

2. Stop the ping pong game and bless your marriage partner even when he is slapping you on the cheek or sinning against you.

3. Stop protecting self and start trusting God.

Winning Your Enemy to Be Your Friend

Sometimes married couples reach a point in relationship in which they are really treating each other much more like enemies than even like friends, let alone husband and wife. Below I have copied excerpts from a letter I wrote to one husband in this situation. This letter contains three key principles that are useful in winning your enemy (spouse) back to be your friend.

Dear Fred,

I would first like to outline three key principles that I know to be true in any spiritual battle that involves other people. I believe that these three principles must be brought to bear in your relating to Lucy...

1. **Respond In the Opposite Spirit:** If one wants to win a spiritual battle, one must always minister and respond in the opposite attitude and spirit to the spirit coming at one. If you wish to intensify a battle, just respond in the same spirit coming at you. Meet cursing with cursing, accusation with accusation. Meet rejection with rejection, pride with pride (justification), abandonment with abandonment, condemnation with condemnation, disloyalty with disloyalty, greed with greed (protection), etc. If you wish to defeat the true enemy (Ephesians 6:12) and

win a spiritual battle, you must meet cursing with blessing, accusation with confession, rejection with acceptance, pride with humility, abandonment with committed support, condemnation with commendation, disloyalty with loyalty, greed with generosity, etc. So, with Lucy, you can respond in the same spirit coming at you or in the opposite spirit.

2. **Respond In Faith** by "calling things that be not, as though they were." Romans 4:17 speaking of God says, "...*even God, Who quickeneth the dead, and calleth those things which be not as though they were.*" This is a classic faith principle I learned years ago that has to do with what I believe is God's method of bringing about change. God speaks and behaves toward people and circumstances that are not yet manifest on earth according to His will, as if these things already were manifest reality. He said to Abraham, "I have made you a father of many nations." Sarah was still barren at the time. Jesus said to the woman bent over with a spirit of infirmity for many years, "Woman you are loosed from your infirmity," while she was still bent over and in bondage (Luke 13:10-13). There are many other examples: "the little girl is not dead, she is just sleeping (Luke 8:52, Mark 3:1-5, etc.).

Man's idea of how to bring about change, on the other hand, is to call those things that be as they are and then try to use logic, reasoning, teaching and programs to convince people to change. This, of course rarely works. Paul uses this faith principle in Romans 12:19-21 where he says, "*Beloved, do not avenge yourselves, but rather give place to wrath; for it is written, 'Vengeance is Mine, I will repay,' says the Lord. Therefore, If your enemy is hungry, feed him; if he is thirsty give him a drink; For in so doing you will heap coals of fire on his head.' Do not be overcome by evil, but overcome evil with good.*"

Paul does not suggest confronting your enemy with the fact that he is acting like an enemy and trying to convince him to stop it. He suggests treating your enemy as if he were a friend. Why? Because this is God's method of change. When you treat the person acting like your enemy as a friend, you by faith are calling things that be not (yet manifest) (i.e. friendship) as though they were (already manifest), thereby transforming your enemy into your friend.

So, with Lucy, you can treat her according to the way you perceive she now is and try to convince her to change, or you can treat her by faith according to the way God has called her to be. If she is acting as your enemy and yet is hungry and thirsty, you could do as scripture suggests, feed her and give her a drink. This would be acting in faith, treating her as your wife and friend when she is not yet acting like your wife and friend. This is God's method of bringing about change in her heart. On the other hand, telling her that you will not feed her or give her a drink until she does what you want is the opposite of faith. It is saying, "I will not act until I see the manifestation I desire first."

Another example of this same principle is recorded in Matthew 5:38-42. Jesus said, *"You have heard that it was said, 'An eye for an eye and a tooth for a tooth.' But I tell you not to resist an evil person. But whoever slaps you on your right cheek, turn the other to him also. If anyone wants to sue you and take away your tunic, let him have your cloak also. And whoever compels you to go one mile, go with him two. Give to him who asks you, and from him who wants to borrow from you do not turn away."* Unbelief says, "I will treat you the way you are treating me." Faith says, " I will unilaterally give to you more than you ask and will treat you as a friend even while you are treating me as an enemy." So my suggestion would be to implement this principle with Lucy and give to her significantly more than she asks.

3. **Love Your Enemies and Bless Those Who Curse You:** Jesus said in Matthew 5:44-47 that there is a special class of people that you should go out of your way to bless: Enemies. *"But I say to you, love your enemies, bless those who curse you, and pray for those who spitefully use you and persecute you, ..."* Certainly you should love and bless your wife, your family and friends. However, it is more difficult when it seems that a wife may be treating you as an enemy. If it is difficult to bless Lucy as a wife, or a friend, then it is very important to at least begin to bless her as an enemy. Bless in Greek is the word "Eulogia." This word primarily means, "to speak well of." Bless in Hebrew is the word "Baruch." This word literally means, "to kneel before." The primary spiritual connotation is "to empower to prosper." Therefore if you were to bless Lucy as your enemy, it would mean that you would kneel before her, empower her to prosper, and speak well of her.

The above three principles outlined in the letter to Fred are universal principles that may be used in restoring any relationship, but particularly a damaged or broken marriage relationship.

My hope in sharing these two letters with you is that if you are in a situation in which you have already significantly wounded your spouse, you might grab hold of these principles and begin to implement them in your own situation.

Reflection

1. It is not the confession of your marriage partner's sins and faults that will bring about the healing spoken of in the book of James.

2. Confession of your own sins to one another and prayer for each other creates the potential that you both might be healed, and your relationship benefited.

3. Stop the ping pong game and bless your marriage partner even when he is not blessing you.

4. Stop protecting yourself, and start trusting God to protect you.

5. Become like David Wilkerson with Nicky Cruz, and allow the death coming from your spouse to pass through you into the death of Christ in order that you might retransmit to your spouse the life of Christ.

6. When your spouse is treating you as an enemy and you wish to win him back to be your friend, respond in the following three ways:

    a. Respond in the opposite spirit to the one coming at you. Meet cursing with blessing, rejection with acceptance, greed with generosity, pride with humility, and so forth.

    b. Respond in faith, calling things that are not (yet manifest) as thought they were.

    c. Love your enemies (your marriage partner) and bless those who curse you.

chapter 11

4 Key Gifts to Restore Covenant in Marriage

et's now return our discussion to some very practical ways in which you can personally restore or renew the protective hedge of covenant around your marriage. Remember that the protective hedge of covenant really is the key to transparent heart-to-heart communication. If I am afraid that my spouse may leave me if I openly share the truly ugly parts of my life, then I will choose to keep these things hidden. Transparency, of course is the key to intimacy. Again, conflict is very difficult to resolve without a willingness to enter into open heart-to-heart communication. So, conflict resolution and true communication are really rooted in the protective hedge of covenant being in place in a marriage.

True covenant can only be implemented by those willing to let go of their fleadom and embrace the freedom of drawing life from God and unconditionally serving a marriage partner. In this chapter we will talk about some of the practical implications of re-establishing the value of covenant in our marriage. It is exemplified by the traditional commitment made by eastern men to each other in the consummating of a blood covenant: "All I have and all I am is yours." Remember that a blood covenant is an unconditional, unilateral promise that is terminated only by death.

We talked in chapter three about seven components of an eastern covenant, all of which are contained in our traditional western wedding ceremony. In review, these seven components are:

1. Unilateral commitment before God
2. Expression of terms and scope of covenant
3. Exchange of four gifts
4. Vows are proclaimed
5. Witnesses are present
6. Phylacteries (tokens) are exchanged
7. A covenant meal is shared.

Rededication of Marriage to Covenant

A very powerful way to reaffirm the covenant of marriage is to **participate in a Covenant Marriage Retreat** conducted by Family Foundations International. For more information on attending such a retreat, see the Appendix and you may look on the Internet website: www.familyfoundations.com. In this retreat, we ask the participants to prepare to exchange with each other in a rededication ceremony the same four gifts that eastern men would exchange when making a blood covenant. I have briefly listed these four gifts in chapter three, but in this chapter I would like to examine them in more detail.

If you are not able to attend a Covenant Marriage Retreat, I would suggest that you each prepare these same gifts and find a time to give them to each other. So as we go through in more detail what each of these four gifts represent, I would encourage you to make your own personal list of what part of each of these gifts you may have been withholding from your spouse and would now like to restore. Ask God to open your eyes to your own fleadom in each of these areas in which you have not been acting as a free person to unconditionally give to your spouse without expectation of return. Then find a time to share your list with your spouse and ask him to forgive you for withholding these things. This would also be a good time to restate your marriage vows to each other and rededicate your marriage to covenant before God and witnesses.

We have found, however, that some couples who have significantly wounded each other, such as Dan and Carol, to whom I wrote the letter in the last chapter, may not yet be ready to honestly exchange these four gifts immediately. It may take some time. Some may need to work more on rebuilding trust and relationship first. However, even if you are not ready yet to honestly give these four gifts to your spouse, I still encourage you to dedicate your own heart to covenant in your marriage, and continue to seek counsel, healing and restoration.

I remember working for over a year with one such couple. Scott had been quite a scoundrel for more than a decade, when he finally gave his life to the Lord. He then asked his wife, Patty, for forgiveness and began to work on restoring communication, trust, and covenant in his marriage. They both wanted to attend a Covenant Marriage Retreat, give these four gifts to each other, and rededicate their marriage to God in covenant.

However, during the preparation time, as Patty made her lists of the four gifts, she told us, "I can't honestly say that I trust either God or Scott enough to really say these things or to relinquish my defensive weapons that I have relied upon for more than a decade to keep myself safe. I know my husband has changed a lot, but I still can't say these words with integrity."

Patty decided that she wanted to wait until more healing had taken place between them and she could honestly say that she would lay her weapons down and leave herself open and vulnerable before her husband. Scott was a little hurt at first, but he realized that he had deeply wounded his wife over the last decade through his alcohol abuse and infidelity, and he was willing to continue to receive counseling and healing and wait to go through the rededication ceremony until she was ready. Patty again reviewed the information in this chapter six months later, as we were having another Covenant Marriage Retreat, but decided that she still wasn't ready. She still didn't feel that she could say these words with integrity.

A year later, the third time we offered the Covenant Marriage Retreat, Patty was finally ready to trust God, and in integrity to offer Scott these four gifts. When they did so, there was a powerful sealing of covenant (like tooth enamel) around their marriage that has made the relationship extremely strong and stable.

There is no doubt that all of us need God's grace in our marriage in order to lay down our weapons and not pick them up again. However, I believe that God honored Patty's integrity not to speak words in a rededication ceremony that she did not mean and couldn't honestly stand behind. Since that time Scott and Patty have become actively involved in teaching classes in their church on covenant marriage, and have worked with many other couples to help bring healing and restoration to broken marriages.

I would like now to look at the significance of each of these four gifts, and suggest how they might apply to our marriages today as we seek to re-establish the protective hedge of covenant. Men would give:

1. Their coats or robes,
2. Their weapon belts and weapons,
3. Their names, and
4. Their own blood.

It is interesting to note that these four critical expressions of personhood that are freely given in covenant are the same four things that are protected in battle. If captured in battle, the conqueror will immediately strip the prisoner of these four expressions of personhood. If you are captured, your captors will take your coat and all of your possessions. They will certainly remove your weapons and weapon belt. They will strip you of your name and you will be known as prisoner #5869351287. Your very life is also then taken or preserved at the sole discretion of your captors. Yet, when blood covenant is consummated, these are the four gifts that are freely given to the blood covenant partner. Thus, the giving of these four gifts in covenant is a very powerful expression of cessation of any hostilities and total surrender to one another.

The Coat or Robe

In making a blood covenant with each other, men would exchange their outer garments, their coats or robes. The coat signifies the rights and possessions and standing within a family, tribe or community. The coat represents all I have. If a man is a military man, his coat is significant of his rank and authority within the military. Within a tribe or family, the coat may bear some family significance. For example, the biblical patriarch, Joseph was given a very special coat, the "coat of many colors" by his father. This coat was apparently very unique and bespoke of a very special standing and relationship with his father, Jacob.

So when a man would give his coat to another in covenant, he was conveying to that blood covenant partner the same standing in his family, tribe or community. He was also conveying to his covenant partner access to any and all of his possessions. In giving the coat, he was saying, "Anything I have is yours if you need it. I will withhold nothing from you. All I have from this time forward is communal property between us both. Relinquishment of the coat also signifies the relinquishment of all rights. "Any rights I have, I give up in your presence."

So when we apply this to the covenant commitment we are re-establishing with each other as a married couple, I am formally saying to my spouse, "I lay my coat at your feet. All I have is yours. All of my possessions from this time forward are available to you. Nothing is mine. Everything is ours. I furthermore give up any personal rights I have held." So, let's look at some of the things that might be represented by the coat in modern times, that would need to be relinquished in reaffirming the covenant of marriage with each other.

What type of possessions do married couples withhold from each other in modern times? Some people withhold money. I have encountered many couples who retain separate bank accounts. Because they don't trust each other, some couples actually hide money and have secret accounts. Obviously, these accounts need to be given up and disclosed when we are in covenant in marriage.

Other people have prized possessions that they withhold from their marriage partner. "This is mine, and I don't want you to touch it." Again this is contract, not covenant.

Willard Harley, in his masterful book *His Needs, Her Needs*[1] has identified ten primary needs of both husbands and wives. They are as follows:

1. Sexual fulfillment
2. Recreational companionship
3. An attractive spouse
4. Domestic support
5. Admiration
6. Affection
7. Conversation
8. Honesty and openness
9. Financial support

[1] Harley, Willard, Jr. Ph.D., *His Needs, Her Needs*, Old Tappan, NJ, Fleming H. Revell Company, 1995

10. Family commitment

These needs then would all be gifts that are to be freely given in covenant marriage. For most flea couples living in a contract marriage, many of these are things that would be withheld or are used as bargaining chips to get a spouse to meet my needs. Please ask the Lord to identify for you which ones of these you have not been freely giving to your spouse.

Another aspect of the coat is that of rights. When I lay my coat at my spouse's feet, I am also laying down all of my rights. What type of rights might one be withholding from a spouse? Some of the rights I thought of are:

1.   The right to control my time as I please
2.   The right to come home when I want
3.   The right to sleep when I want to
4.   The right to maintain a reputation
5.   The right to be treated fairly
6.   The right to control my own money as I please
7.   The right to be happy

Obviously neither of these are exhaustive lists. As you read and think about these lists, there may be several other rights or possessions that may come to your mind. I encourage you to make a list and then seek the Lord as to how you might trust Him with these rights and possessions, so that you would not be in need of protecting these things from your spouse as a flea, but rather would be free to give these things to your spouse as a gift as you reaffirm your covenant of marriage.

The Weapon Belt and Weapons

Laying weapons and a weapon belt at another person's feet is a very obvious sign of surrender and cessation of hostilities. When an eastern man would lay his weapon belt at another's feet, he was signifying, "I give you all my strength and military might. I will never again use these weapons against you. I will never fight for me against you. From now on, I will only fight for us, but never for me. Your enemies are my enemies. Furthermore, I lay myself completely open and naked before you. If you want to harm or kill me, I will not defend myself against you." In order to do this, it again requires a trust in God for protection rather than a trust in myself and my weapons.

In ancient times, men would use swords, knives, spears and shields. In modern times people arm themselves with guns, knives, tanks and bombs. Most married couples don't utilize many of these weapons against each other. (However, I have known a few who have.) So what would be more typical weapons that husbands and wives would use against each other today? Below is a list of some that I thought of.

1. Withholding of money
2. Withholding of sex
3. Isolation
4. Criticism
5. Dishonor
6. Fits of rage and anger
7. Unforgiveness
8. Bitterness
9. Threats
10. Self pity
11. Crying
12. Shame
13. Manipulation
14. Bribes
15. Hardening of heart

Again this is not an exhaustive list. What type of offensive weapons do you use when you are threatened or hurt? What type of defensive weapons do you use when attacked? These are all things that we want to lay at one another's feet as we re-establish the protective hedge of covenant in marriage.

The first two listed above are quite common. Frequently a husband will control money and only release money to his wife if she does what he wants. In retaliation, the wife will withhold sexual relationship unless he does what she wants and releases money to her. Now we have a classic relationship of prostitution taking place within this marriage. "I'll give you money if you give me sex." Obviously this is not covenant and is certainly not what God intended for marriage to be. Furthermore, it creates a very unpleasant experience for both husband and wife.

The Name = Power of Attorney

When eastern men made a covenant, they would exchange their names. To give another person your name is very powerful as the name represents the person and his authority. To convey to another your name is to convey power of attorney. When you give someone your name, you have given him the right to be your representative and to exercise authority on your behalf.

For example, suppose Bill Gates, a very wealthy man, gave you his name and the legal right (power of attorney) to use it. If this were indeed authorized by Bill and given to you, you could then walk into the bank in which Bill Gates keeps his accounts and request of the teller to give you 10 million dollars. The teller might ask you, "Who are you?" You would then respond, "It doesn't really matter who I am, because I come to you in the name of Bill Gates. My name doesn't matter. Only his does in this bank, and he has given me power of attorney to use his name. So, when I speak to you, it is the same as if Bill himself were here speaking to you." The teller would then verify the authenticity of the document, and if it were indeed valid, he would then grant you the 10 million dollars.

Many people would love to have a letter authorizing them with a general power of attorney from Bill Gates. However, most people have never thought about the fact that if they have entered into covenant with Almighty God by stepping across the threshold of His dwelling by the blood of Jesus Christ, they have been given power of attorney to use His name. Most people simply use "in the name of Jesus" as the concluding statement of a prayer without realizing that they are actually speaking in His stead as His covenant representative on earth. Maybe people would be more careful what they prayed in Jesus' name if they had a better understanding of the power of attorney granted by their covenant authority.

So when I make a covenant and I grant my covenant partner the right to use my name, I really make her my representative and I am granting her the power of attorney to speak and act on my behalf. This is actually what you have already done with your spouse on your wedding day.

In the book of Genesis in the Bible, when God made a covenant with Abram, He exchanged names with him. Abram's name was changed to Abraham. I am told that the "ah" that was inserted into Abram's name was a part of God's name. The "ah" part became a part of Abram's name as it was changed from Abram to Abraham," thus making Abraham God's representative on earth and granting him God's authority. Even more incredible is that God forever after also took on Abraham's name in that He has been known since that covenant was cut as "the God of Abraham."

It is common custom in marriage in most western countries for the groom to give his surname (last, or family name) to his bride. In so doing, he is granting her the power of attorney to speak and act in his behalf. She has the same authority, rights and privileges that he does when she receives his name. So in restoring our marriage to covenant it is good to think about and ask the Lord to expose any areas in which either spouse has misused the name (power, authority, representation) of the other or has failed to back up what the other said or did. We want to expose any areas in which we have begun to operate independently of each other, denying the fact that we are one and have granted to each other power of attorney by covenant to represent each other privately or publicly.

Blood = Life

When men in the East would enter into blood covenant, the verb to "cut" the covenant was frequently used. The reason for this is that frequently the covenant was consummated by the shedding and commingling of each other's blood. Most of the time in a western culture, when we think of blood, we immediately think of death. However, in the eastern mind, blood represents life.

"For it is the life of all flesh. Its blood sustains its life. Therefore I said to the children of Israel, 'You shall not eat the blood of any flesh, for the life of all flesh is its blood. Whoever eats it shall be cut off'" (Leviticus 17:14).

We see in this scripture that the clear idea in the Bible is that the life of any being is contained in its blood. God forbade the Hebrew people to eat the blood of animals because He did not want them to partake of the nature, character and life of those animals. However other eastern men would frequently consummate a covenant by shedding and drinking each other's blood, thereby receiving the very life of the other and becoming one. Offering a covenant partner your blood signifies a willingness to give up your life for that covenant partner.

> Offering a covenant partner your blood signifies a willingness to give up your life for that covenant partner.

Jesus Christ utilized this same concept in John chapter six when He stated:

"Most assuredly I say to you, unless you eat the flesh of the Son of Man and drink His blood, you have no life in you. Whoever eats My flesh and

drinks my blood has eternal life and I will raise him up at the last day. For my flesh is food indeed and my blood is drink indeed. He who eats My flesh and drinks My blood abides in Me and I in Him" (John 6:53-56).

Most Christians have partaken of communion, or the Lord's Supper, but have never correlated it with the eastern concept of covenant. When we are receiving communion, we are acknowledging the covenant we have with God by the shed blood of Jesus. He has made a covenant commitment to us and has made us His ambassadors and representatives.

Although I would not suggest that you reaffirm your marriage covenant by commingling each other's physical blood, I would suggest that you express your willingness to die for your spouse. This not only includes a willingness to physically die, but also to die to your own selfishness. This is sometimes more difficult than dying physically. Ask the Lord to show you in what areas you have sought to preserve your own life, physically or emotionally at the expense of your spouse.

I would then suggest that you make a list of these areas and ask your marriage partner to forgive you. Then express your willingness to give up your own blood (life) for the sake of your spouse.

In the Covenant Marriage Retreat we conduct, we conclude the retreat with a ceremony to rededicate our marriages to covenant with each other before God. I would suggest that you find a time to either attend one of these retreats as a couple, or to have a ceremony in which you convey these four gifts to each other. We have found that periodically reviewing these four gifts given in covenant is very helpful. Jan and I found personally that the first time we rededicated our marriage to the Lord in covenant, even though we understood and committed our marriage to covenant on our wedding day, that over a period of time, we had begun to withhold from each other various rights, and possessions and use various weapons against each other.

When we then laid all of these things down in our first rededication ceremony, we thought that we would never need to do so again. However, a couple of years later when we asked the Lord the questions again about what rights, possessions, weapons, and unwillingness to die for each other had again crept into our relationship, we were surprised to find that several of these things needed to be cleaned out again. So, we have found that it is very helpful to periodically review these four covenant gifts of coats, weapons, name and blood in our own marriage in order to discover how we have slipped back into contract thinking in some of these areas again. We can then relinquish these things to each other and clean out these areas of our relationship. In this way, we are continually growing in relationship and intimacy and allowing God to make our marriage more a picture of Christ and His bride every day.

Reflection

1. Four key gifts are exchanged by eastern men when they make a blood covenant, signifying, "All I have, and all I am is yours."

2. The coat signifies:

    a. My Rights.

    b. My Possessions.

3. The weapon belt and weapons signify:

    a. Offensive weapons.

    b. Defensive weapons.

4. My name signifies my power of attorney.

    a. When my name is conveyed to my spouse, I have given him power of attorney as a covenant partner to act in my stead.

    b. I will back up whatever my spouse says in my name.

5. My blood signifies my very life.

a. Giving of my blood signifies my willingness to die for my spouse.

b. My willingness to die is not only physical, but also a willingness to die to my own will, desires, and selfishness.

6. Are you willing and prepared to give these four gifts to your spouse in a renewed commitment of your marriage to covenant?

Resources

[1] *An Ancient Paths Seminar*: Covenant Marriage (Covenant Marriage Retreat). See Appendix for details and www.familyfoundations.com for schedule of upcoming events.

🎧 Blood Covenant 1 and 2

conclusion

We have found that if a married couple is able to effectively put in place the three key principles outlined in this book and function in them as free people rather than fleas, they will have a very pleasant and fulfilling journey through life. If not, unfortunately marriage may feel more like an endurance contest. If a couple is able to utilize **conflict** to remove viruses in each other's lives and become more free each time, then conflict becomes an opportunity for growth in intimacy and emotional maturity rather than an emotionally painful and destructive event.

Conflict is certainly much easier to resolve when a couple has become aware of relational communication messages, spiritual warfare and the schemes of the devil operating within their own marriage. Such awareness is much more likely to be present when a couple has established a strong foundation of regular, intimate, transparent heart to heart **communication** and prayer.

This foundation of transparency and intimacy is then much easier to establish when the protective hedge of **covenant** is in place and the life-long security of the marriage relationship is intact.

Underlying these three principles of **covenant, communication and conflict resolution** is, of course, the fact that a couple must be living for a **purpose and destiny greater than self** and personal happiness. If the highest purpose in the marriage is personal pleasure, pain avoidance, and fulfillment of self, then both husband and wife will most likely struggle for most of their marriage in an emotionally painful, unfulfilled state of being two fleas. Thus it is critical for a couple to be focused on pleasing God, finding His purpose for their lives and marriage, and be striving together in unity as a team to accomplish their God-given destiny.

As you not only read and understand, but actually implement and practice the principles and exercises described in this book, I believe that you will experience more and more of the fulfillment and pleasure that God intended for your marriage. It is Jan's and my sincere desire that every couple reading this book may find themselves quickly out of the water and up in the canoe paddling together as a team toward their destiny.

I remember hearing about the response of one very successful man, who when asked about the key to his success, pondered for a moment and then said, **"Get started, and don't quit."** We suggest this same strategy for successfully moving your marriage forward to the next stage. Success in any area of life is not usually obtained through the discovery of one huge key, but rather through the consistent, daily practice of a few simple habits.

If you're not sure where to start, let me suggest initiating a habit of praying together as a couple face to face just five minutes every day as I described in chapter seven. You can't go wrong by daily humbling yourselves, blessing each other and asking for God's help in your lives and marriage. Once this habit is regularly in place, you may choose to work on another principle or a practice to put in place. So, if you will get started and not quit, it is Jan's and my sincere belief that no matter where you begin, you will find yourselves in a relatively short period of time sitting together in your canoe paddling in sync towards your destiny. **We know you can and will, with God's help, transform your marriage from fleadom to freedom!**

appendix

about
the author

Craig Hill and his wife, Jan, live near Denver, Colorado, U.S.A. Craig and Jan give senior leadership to Family Foundations International (FFI). FFI is a non-profit Christian ministry through which life-changing seminars are conducted in many nations of the world. Craig has written several books, including his best seller, *The Ancient Paths.*

Through his past experience in business, missions, counseling and pastoral ministry, God has given Craig unique insight into marriage, family, financial and interpersonal relationships. This has resulted in his ability to identify for many people, root causes of relational conflict, compulsive habits, low self-esteem, workaholism, lack of financial provision and other undesirable life patterns, which are repeated from one generation to the next.

By interweaving personal stories with biblical truths, God has anointed Craig to pierce through the veil of the mind to minister to the depths of the heart, resulting in real life change for many.

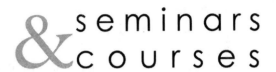

seminars & courses

Family Foundations International

Embracing God's Ancient Paths of Blessing—
An Experience of the Heart You'll Never Forget!

Family Foundations (FFI) is a non-profit Christian ministry, based out of Colorado, USA. FFI provides seminars and other tools through local churches and businesses in many countries around the world. Craig & Jan Hill are the founders of FFI.

The Ancient Paths Seminars give solid biblical principles, and Craig Hill's moving examples open the heart for participants to receive truth and rest for their souls. The intent of the teaching is not just for information, but to touch the heart. This often exposes hidden areas of woundedness that have occurred in the participant's life. The small group times allow participants to seek and receive God's powerful truth and light in these areas.

For a schedule of seminars or to locate the FFI office nearest you, go to www.familyfoundations.com. Seminars are available through FFI Seminar Coordinators. Courses are available for purchase.

SEMINARS

An Ancient Paths Seminar: EMPOWERING RELATIONSHIPS

Empowering Relationships is a teaching and small group seminar on relationships. This 12-hour seminar includes the following topics:

- Relational versus Topical Communication
- Winning the Battle Over Destructive Attitudes, Habits and Behavior
- Removing Roots That Damage or Destroy Relationships
- Understanding and Breaking Eight Negative Adult Life Patterns

An Ancient Paths Seminar: BLESSING GENERATIONS

Blessing Generations is a teaching and small group seminar on the power of blessing in seven critical times in life. In this 12-hour seminar, participants learn and experience the power of the blessing as the single most important factor that empowers people to prosper. Come learn and apply the blessing in your life.

Topics include

- Seven Critical Times of Blessing in Our Lives
- Consequences of the Lack of Blessing
- Impartation of the Father's Blessing
- The Power Behind Your Name

THE ANCIENT PATHS SEMINAR

The Ancient Paths Seminar is the original 16-hour seminar including the topics of both Empowering Relationships and Blessing Generations Seminars in a condensed format.

An Ancient Paths Seminar: COVENANT MARRIAGE
(Covenant Marriage Retreat)

Married couples come to understand God's heart for their marriage, the true meaning of covenant and the power of a covenant commitment!

Learn how to add intimacy and unity as a couple and how to divorce-proof your marriage. The weekend ends in a covenant vows renewal ceremony where many couples realize for the first time the power of the covenant words in the vows they speak, sealing their marriage for life. Topics include:

- Communication in Marriage
- How to divorce-proof your marriage
- Intimacy through transparency
- How to realistically function in unity
- Understanding God's heart, His perfect way, for your marriage
- Why the Biblical view on blood covenant and the threshold covenant are critical to your marriage
- How marriage and covenant reflect the image of God

An Ancient Paths Seminar: OVERCOMING ANGER

Overcoming Anger is a seminar that presents practical, biblically-based reasons for anger and solutions to overcome anger and other compulsive habits in people's lives. Topics include:

- The Anger Cycle
- Why do I do what I don't want to do?
- Identifying the real source of anger and frustration
- Removing the power of people and circumstances to control my life
- Three key steps to overcoming anger

An Ancient Paths Seminar: TRANSFORMING HEARTS

This is a follow-up (level 2) seminar, which may be attended following any seminar with small group ministry.

Topics include:

- The authority of the believer
- Freedom from shame
- Softening the hardened heart
- Refocus on who I am in Christ

An Ancient Paths Seminar: FINANCIAL SUCCESS

This seminar is different from many Christian finance seminars. The teaching does not feature merely "practical" information on finances, but follows Craig Hill's anointed understanding of God's Word in teaching finances from a biblical and heart perspective (Matt. 6:21).

Topics include:

- Discover the difference between wealth, riches and money
- What is "Mammon?"
- Learn a systemized guide to getting out of debt
- Learn five scriptural uses of money
- Learn how to release God's blessing in finances

An Ancient Paths Seminar: THE QUESTION

This is an exciting and life-changing teaching and audio/video presentation designed specially for young men and young women but found to open hearts of men and women of all ages. The Question (a 12-hour event) includes thought provoking teaching on video and sharing, prayer and Holy Spirit-led ministry to the heart in small groups. There are two separate versions of The Question, one for women and one for men.